Celebrating Initiation

A Guide for Priests

SECOND EDITION

Fountain
of Life SERIES

Paul Turner

017189

World Library Publications
the music and liturgy division of J. S. Paluch Company, Inc.
3708 River Road, Suite 400 • Franklin Park, IL 60131-2158
800 566-6150 • wlpmusic.com

Celebrating Initiation

A Guide for Priests

SECOND EDITION

WLP 017189

ISBN 978-1-58459-341-6

Author: Paul Turner
Editor: Jerry Galipeau
Copy Editor: Marcia T. Lucey
Design and Typesetting: Chris Broquet and Denise C. Durand
Cover photo: Copyright © John Zich. Used by permission.

Fourth Printing
Excerpts from the English translation of *Rite of Baptism for Children* © 1969,
International Commission on English in the Liturgy Corporation (ICEL); excerpts
from the English translation of *The Roman Missal* © 2010, International Commission
on English in the Liturgy Corporation (ICEL); excerpts from the English translation of
Rite of Christian Initiation of Adults © 1985, ICEL. All rights reserved.

I wish to thank . . .

Jerry Galipeau and Mary Beth Kunde-Anderson,

who asked

Rita Ferrone and George Smiga,

who critiqued

the North American Forum on the Catechumenate,

which inspired

the people of St. Munchin and St. Aloysius,

who celebrate

God, who begins and ends.

PT

Table of Contents

Introduction

Your ordination to the priesthood was one of the most important events in your life. You probably remember the anniversary and celebrate it every year. Still, your baptism was even more significant, even if you were too young to remember it. On that day you began sharing life in Christ.

Now as a priest you administer baptism. Initiation is probably one of your most satisfying ministries. Celebrating Mass is always a privilege. Funerals can be heart-wrenching. Weddings present unique challenges for sacred ritual. Confessions range from the superficial to the poignant. But the initiation rites almost always celebrate a time of great joy and welcome.

There are exceptions. Some newly-baptized adults rarely return to church. Some parents disappear after the baptism of their children. Some First Communions are last Communions.

Still, joyful events put initiation into motion. New life has come to a young family. A spouse decides to seek baptism. Children open their eyes to God as they prepare for First Communion.

The priest humbly finds himself at the exciting crossroads between an inviting God and a responding believer. His task is to celebrate the rites in a way that facilitates this divine communication. A good presider becomes transparent to the words and actions of initiation. He watches, guides, and channels God's love.

I have written this book for my brother priests. Deacons may benefit from it because they also preside for many of these rites. Lay ministers may enjoy reading over my shoulder. But I have written this book primarily for priests to explain the many rites we need to know, and to help integrate them into the particular work we do as pastors, presiders, and preachers.

I hope this book will deepen your understanding of the rites of initiation over which you preside. These include the following: the Christian Initiation of Adults (*RCIA*), the Reception of Baptized Christians into the Full Communion of the Catholic Church, Baptism for Children (*RBC*), Confirmation (*RC*), First Communion, and parts of Pastoral Care of the Sick (*PCS*). This book will survey the ritual, the rules, and the options while making suggestions for fruitful celebrations.

I am deeply indebted to the North American Forum on the Catechumenate (www.naforum.org). Its vision has shaped many, though not all, of my thoughts about presiding for the catechumenate rites. The Forum's catechists and liturgists have taught me many valuable insights and challenged me to think of these rites in vigorous ways. Many of the ideas in this book germinate from my work with the Forum, though I diverge from time to time. This book is not intended to represent the Forum's point of view; it portrays my thoughts as a presider experienced in sin and grace, schooled by the history of the catechumenate and by contemporary catechists.

As one priest to another, I assure you of my prayers for your work and my admiration for the gift of your service to the Church. As you celebrate initiation with the people of God, may you be filled with the spirit of wonder and awe in God's presence; see *RCIA* 234.

Acceptance into the
Order of Catechumens
(RCIA 48–74)

When you have *unbaptized* adults asking for the sacraments, you formally hear and accept their intentions in the ceremony called the Rite of Acceptance into the Order of Catechumens (*RCIA* 41–68). It marks the beginning of their preparation for baptism.

(If these adults have already been baptized, see my treatment of the Rite of Welcoming the Candidates on p. 36. If you have a mixed group of unbaptized and baptized candidates, see p. 43.)

Your group may include unbaptized children of catechetical age. The *Code of Canon Law* (*CCL*) says that children are considered "adults" if they are no longer infants and have attained the use of reason (852/1). This designation relates *only to baptism*, not to the other sacraments. Obviously, a child with the use of reason is not an adult as far as marriage is concerned. The dividing line for baptism is called "catechetical age" in *RCIA* 252. If parents request sacraments for a child old enough to prepare for First Communion, but who has never been baptized, that child belongs in the catechumenate. The ritual book that guides this initiation is not the *Rite of Baptism for Children*, but the *Rite of Christian Initiation of Adults*.

(For children younger than catechetical age, see my comments on the *Rite of Baptism for Children* on p. 139.)

Ordinarily, do not omit this ceremony. The Catholic Church includes an "order" of catechumens. We pray for them each year during the Good Friday liturgy. If they are engaged, they may have a Catholic wedding (*RCIA* 47). If they die, they are entitled to Christian burial (*CCL* 1183). Most importantly, this ceremony gives them their identity, and it establishes their relationship with the universal and local church.

There are exceptional circumstances when the rite of acceptance is folded into the same ceremony with baptism (*RCIA* 341–345; 377–378), or when it is omitted because death is imminent (373). But by design these circumstances are not the norm.

The very existence of the rite of acceptance presumes you are an evangelizer. When you meet people who are unbaptized, invite them to know Christ and to give themselves to him. Many people are waiting for an invitation, and you are in a unique position to extend it. Stay alert when people drop clues that they are missing something in their lives. You might be the instrument that brings these inquirers to Christ.

To prepare for this celebration, get to know those who are beginning their Christian formation in your parish. Be sure you know the sponsors, which ones are pairing up with which inquirers, and why.

Discerning readiness is essential. This rite is for those inquirers who are ready for the order of catechumens. Someone has to discern this. That someone may be you, or it may be your catechumenate director, team, and sponsors. Some concrete decision needs to be reached.

The criteria for readiness are outlined in *RCIA* 42. Evaluate the potential catechumens according to their spiritual life, their grasp of Christian teachings, evidence of faith, the intention to change their lives, and their relationship with God in Christ. They should have a start on repentance and prayer, a sense of Church, and some experience with the Christian community. They don't need to have absorbed all these areas in depth; it suffices to have the "first" of this, the "initial" of that, a "sense" of something else, and "some" of something more. But you should know that these persons have started down the path of all they need to be Christian: spirit, understanding, community, and a relationship with Christ. It's tempting to judge readiness based on attendance: if the inquirers have been showing up for sessions, we assume they are ready. That might hold, but it might not. Look a little deeper. Get a sense of who the inquirers are and how they are doing. They deserve attention case by case.

You will ask the inquirers some questions during the ceremony. They may prepare their responses beforehand. You or someone from your team could help them know what to say and when.

It will also help if you rehearse the sponsors. You may rehearse with the inquirers, too, but the sponsor should guide them through the ceremony. It is usually all right if the inquirers come a little nervous, as long as the sponsors can confidently guide them through the stages of the ceremony.

You may schedule this celebration more than once a year (*RCIA* 18/3 and 44). Many parishes run their catechumenate on a school-year model: they begin in the fall and they conclude in the spring. The *RCIA* has a different model in mind: You deal with inquirers as the Holy Spirit prompts them. So, if you have people ready for the rite of acceptance in the fall, fine. Celebrate it in the fall. But if another group connects later and is ready in spring or summer, celebrate this rite a second or third time in the year.

A deacon may lead this rite if you do not (45). There is no provision for a lay person to preside for it.

Personally, I like to incorporate the rite of acceptance into Sunday Mass, but to be honest, it is permissible to arrange it at a word service apart from the Eucharist (*RCIA* 44). The rubrics say it takes place with "a group of the faithful"—as if the full Sunday assembly is not there (48). The priest or deacon may wear a cope, but no mention is made of a chasuble or dalmatic (48). The Missal has no texts for the rite of acceptance; it assumes that this ceremony will take place apart from Mass.

Still, many parishes have celebrated this liturgy well during a regularly scheduled Sunday Mass. It will lengthen the celebration, but if it is carefully prepared and executed, your people will welcome this addition to their repertoire of prayer.

Choose a Mass at which nothing else is going on. You know how difficult this can be in a parish where Sundays may bring infant baptism, scout awards, catechist recognition, a letter from the bishop, or an appeal for a second collection. One year I discovered too late that I had mistakenly scheduled a rite of acceptance on the day we were giving the St. Blaise blessing of throats. It can be done, but these events deserve to be highlighted separately.

Let parishioners know a week in advance through the bulletin and the Sunday announcements. It will prepare them mentally for a longer Mass and dispose their hearts to pray for the inquirers.

Let me take you through this service step by step. It is a complicated liturgy, and it will demand that you think on your feet. Get out your copy of the *RCIA*—preferably the one you will actually have in front of you when you preside for this celebration. Let's examine what it says, beginning at paragraph 48. (Throughout this book, I'll give you my commentary according to the paragraph numbers of the rite in question. I'm assuming you will look at two books at once.)

48. The ceremony begins outside the church, where the candidates and others have gathered. The word "candidates" here means the inquirers: those who are going to become catechumens. It does not refer to baptized candidates, who are considered in the parallel rite of welcoming; see p. 36.

You may wear an alb or a surplice, and a stole. You may also wear a cope of festive color. But this envisions that you are celebrating this liturgy apart from Mass. If you are starting Sunday Mass with this rite, wear a chasuble.

The candidates, their sponsors, and the faithful should already be in place before you get there. Just where that place is depends on your church. Is there room outside the building? That makes the best choice. Do you have a sizeable narthex? You may go there instead. If these locations are inadequate, the ceremony may take place behind the back seats, inside the front door. You may begin "elsewhere"—in the sanctuary or even at some place completely apart from the church. The main symbol here is crossing the threshold of the church. Ideally, you want to greet the candidates outside, begin the ceremony there, and then move the entire group inside for the Liturgy of the Word. Other arrangements are permitted, but they compromise this symbolic intent.

Select the place after considering the architecture, space, the number of people, and the weather. Keep visibility and audibility in mind, too. You want everyone to see what is happening and to hear what the candidates say. You may need sound reinforcement and someone to hold a microphone in front of those who will speak.

By the way, this rite first entered liturgical history with the *Gelasian Sacramentary* and the *Gothic Missal*. Both were compiled by the eighth century, and they preserve formulas that were composed centuries earlier. So, this liturgy is not a new-fangled concoction. It stands in the stream of a long Catholic tradition.

In reality, on a Sunday, it is hard to get people to gather someplace else before they take their seat. On Palm Sunday and the Easter Vigil, for example, if people have already entered the church when you are trying to start Mass outside, it would take a bulldozer to dislodge them. Still, an effort can be made.

Several minutes before the scheduled time of this Mass, you, the cantor, the director of the catechumenate, or some credible speaker could step up to a microphone (preferably not at the ambo, which should be reserved for the Liturgy of the Word.) There a friendly announcement could be made, such as, "Good morning, everyone. Our parish has been supporting several unbaptized people who are beginning to make their commitment to Christ. They are asking for our prayer and support. I invite you now to come outside with me to meet these people, hear from them directly, and offer them your prayers."

Do not process in as usual, but go to the place where the inquirers are. Mass begins at the appointed time in the space outside the church.

Some parishes make that announcement after the opening hymn instead. Imagine it this way: While the inquirers and sponsors are standing outside, you process in as usual during the opening song, make the sign of the cross, greet the people, and then introduce the director of the catechumenate, who explains the rite. The deacon or you should then invite people outside. The cross-bearer walks back out, and people leave their places and process to the inquirers. If everyone sings a song, it will create an atmosphere of joy, care or anticipation. This takes more time than the first way, but it strengthens the meaning of the rite.

It works either way. Try it and see what works for you, but the sooner you establish a pattern with this ritual, the more easily people will know what to expect and the more willing they will be to join the procession out.

You may be thinking, "It'll never work. They won't budge." But try it. You may be surprised. I have been pastor of both urban and rural parishes, and I find that people are more open to this than you may think. What follows can be gripping, and people will be inspired by the faith of those who want to follow Christ.

The opening song can be brief. It just needs to gather the people and set the tone for Mass. I normally recommend singing all the verses of an opening hymn, but you could shorten it on this day. The ceremony itself will help gather and focus the worshiping assembly.

Oh, one other thing. Some communities have started this ritual by having the catechumens knock on the outside door of the church. Inside, the priest says something less campy than "Now, who could that be?" and invites everyone out to greet the newcomers. This is not a good idea. This ritual is not about people on the outside asking to come in, but about the Holy Spirit knocking on the hearts of everyone—inside and out—to reform the community. Besides, the knocking on the door is a sad commentary on how Catholics typically evangelize. While other Christians take out ads, place phone calls, and even go door-to-door inviting people to meet Christ, Catholics sit in the office or at home and wait for the phone to ring or the computer to announce they've got mail. That's not evangelization. Evangelization is getting out of our pew and inviting people to meet Christ on the streets, in the workplace, and at the community pool. If your faith means something to you, you will want others to share it.

49. Once everyone has assembled, you greet the candidates "in a friendly manner." The same expression occurs in the rite of penance (41) and the rite of marriage (19). The rubrics have some fear that we might not be friendly. You then speak to everyone in your own words about the joy of the Church and about your knowledge of the spiritual journey the candidates have already taken. This presumes you know a little about that journey. Your words should be sincere, stemming from your own experience with these people. Keep it brief. There are many more words to come. And see 50 below for another idea.

You invite the sponsors and candidates forward. Meanwhile, everyone may sing an appropriate song. However, this song is not essential, and it might not work. The music is meant to cover the action of getting the candidates into place and to give them some encouragement. The recommended psalm (63) expresses one's longing, thirsting, and pining for God. Sung well, it could bring to light the inner feelings of the candidates. Sung poorly, it may trip a lengthy ceremony as it leaves the starting blocks. If the candidates are already in place during the opening song, there is no need for additional music.

I have the sponsors stand next to their candidates with a hand on their shoulder throughout this next part. While the dialogue happens, this gesture lets the candidates know that someone is right there, watching out for them. It also models for the members of the assembly the care that they too should offer.

50. The opening dialogue names the candidates and expresses their desire. You have several options for this. You may ask for each name individually. Or you may ask once and have them respond one after the other. Or you may do a roll call: Call out their names and have them each respond, "Present."

In many parishes another option is introduced based on the rubrics' invitation to do something similar. You introduce the *sponsor*, who introduces the candidate. A catechist could also make the introductions; see *RCIA* 16. In this case, you would say less about the candidates in your introductory comments (49), and let the sponsors speak on their behalf here. This method of naming of the candidate seems more socially conventional.

The dialogue continues as you ask some meaty questions: What are you asking the Church? What will this do for you? These are great questions, and it would be wise for the candidates to spend considerable time before the ceremony preparing their response. Have them think and pray over this in the days before the ritual. What *are* they asking the Church? This is one reason the congregation listens to this dialogue. They are the Church. They need to know what is being asked of them. The rite suggests the candidates respond with a cool, detached word: "Faith." But deeper responses could be given: "I want to know Christ better." "I want a community to support me when I'm down." "I want one religion to share with my family." "I want more meaning in my life."

Upon hearing the response to the first question, you probe a little deeper. The candidate has just explained what he or she wants; now you ask why. "What does Christ offer you?" "Why do you need the help of a community?" "What will one religion do for your family?" "How will more meaning improve your life?" If the candidates have thought through their responses, this dialogue will be intense. People in the congregation will want to hear every word, and they should. Look the candidates in the eye. Keep the focus of the dialogue between the two of you, even though you are in a very public place. The results will infuse this ceremony with spirit and life.

Other questions may be used. Some parishes have chosen these: "What are you asking God?" And then, "What are you asking the Church?" This pair also works, as long as the candidates explain what they want and why. Some candidates do better if they can respond to just one combined question. In answering what they are seeking, they may explain more deeply what that goal will offer them.

51. In unusual circumstances, the next piece of this ritual may be replaced with a rite of exorcism and renunciation of false worship. Ordinarily, don't do this. Centuries ago, this ritual used to include an exorcism and renunciation. It distanced new Christians from pagan and demonic practices. But the ceremony became controversial because we started exorcising Jews, Muslims, and Protestants, while asking them to renounce their former way of life. The ecumenical and interfaith dialogues have prompted a more respectful approach toward others' religious beliefs; see 72. We no longer presume that all those who are unbaptized have previously been worshiping the devil.

But, who knows? You may some day have an inquirer who frequently engaged in satanic ritual. If so, you could appeal to your bishop for permission to include the exorcism and renunciation as part of this rite. Ordinarily, though, don't do it.

52. You ask the candidates if they accept the gospel, and they promise to follow it. You start with a catechetical summary, a proclamation of something that God does. You situate the candidates' journey in the plan of God. Then you ask the candidates to follow Christ.

The *RCIA* gives you three examples of what to say, but it allows you to use different words, and it encourages you to make up your answers based on the responses you received in the opening dialogue. If you can think on your feet, you will love the possibilities. Even though candidates have rehearsed what they will say in the dialogue, they sometimes say something else as the Spirit prompts them. In your response to this dialogue, you proclaim something about God, a message that addresses whatever the candidates are seeking. You thus make the candidates' acceptance of the gospel all the more appealing. You show how the gospel is what they have been seeking all along.

I like to do this with the individual candidates, not as a group. Immediately after each candidate has finished his or her dialogue with me (50), I prepare my response. I pray silently that God will help me find the right words to say, words that will affirm and challenge. As a prelude to the signing of the candidates, I ask the cross-bearer to step up to the candidate before I begin my address. I have the sponsor take the candidates' hands and place them on the cross, holding them there in a gesture of support and guidance. I also place my hands over theirs, all of us grasping the shaft of the cross, while the candidate gazes on the corpus of Christ. I address the candidate by name.

Then I improvise something based on what I've just heard that candidate say. For example, suppose the candidate has said, "I want one faith in my family so that we will be more united in our home." I might respond with something like this: "N., at the Last Supper Jesus prayed for his disciples to be one. He knew from experience that they sometimes disagreed with each other, and at other times they disappointed him. But he wanted unity. He wanted them to be united with one another, and united with his Father. God is already speaking to your heart, and God wants a deeper union with you. Are you prepared to accept the love of God and follow the gospel of Christ?"

The candidate responds, "I am," which constitutes the first acceptance of the gospel. Everyone sings a short acclamation to express joy and support. Then I go to the next candidate, introduce the sponsor, conduct the dialogue, grasp the cross, formulate the question, and hear his or her first acceptance of the gospel. Everyone sings. I repeat this sequence throughout the group.

If you are not good at improvising, you may use one of the options from the book. You may do it one by one, or just once for the whole group. In that case all the candidates may respond together. But personalizing the dialogue makes this liturgy more expressive. Remember, visibility and audibility are important. Stand the candidates where people can see them; mic the candidates so people can hear them.

53. The sponsors and the assembly express their support. You ask them as a group, and they respond. The rubrics let us do this "in these or similar words," so I break this into two questions. I ask the sponsors for their help, and then I ask the full assembly if they will pray for the candidates and give them good example. All respond affirmatively.

This brief dialogue leads to a prayer—the first time you address God aloud in this liturgy. The prayer never makes a request; it simply gives thanks for what God is doing. It ends with an acclamation: "We praise you, Lord, and we bless you." People will not spontaneously know that they are supposed to repeat this after you. Either they need a handout explaining it, a rehearsal before Mass, or a cantor or commentator who helps them along. This works best if you sing the prayer, which concludes with the same words the people use in their response. I usually recite the prayer up until that point, and then sing the last line. Then the cantor and choir lead everyone to repeat the words and notes I just sang. Once you've done it a few times, people will catch on. It takes a few years to build this tradition, but it can be done.

54. You sign the candidates with the cross. You have choices regarding who does the signing, whether or not the candidates are touched, and how many of the senses are signed. If you are in a culture where touching is taboo, your bishop may permit the signations to be made in the air in front of the candidate. This permission was included during the postconciliar development of this rite because of hesitations among some Asian critics, but in many cultures, there is no problem with this ritual touch.

55. The candidates' forehead is signed, but you have choices for doing it, depending on the number of candidates. In option A, you invite them and their sponsors forward. Actually, this won't be necessary because they already came forward in 49. They come to you one by one, and you trace the sign of the cross on their forehead while saying the appropriate text. If no other senses will be signed, the sponsor also traces the cross on the candidate's forehead. Then everyone sings or says an acclamation in praise of Christ. This sequence is repeated for each candidate.

In option B, for a great many candidates, you address them as a group and make a sign of the cross over all of them together, as you do for the blessing near the end of a typical Mass. No forehead is touched. You recite the appropriate text, and all sing an acclamation. Option B carries footnotes about the possibility that these inquirers have been false worshipers whom you just exorcised. It envisions a society where satanic worship is common, and where conversions to Christ are quite numerous. You may recite the texts once over the whole group, but option A is the more normal choice.

56. Another option may be inserted. Catechists or sponsors sign the candidates on other senses, while you recite a text. Actually, these are body parts, not senses, but the ritual is probably trying to be discreet. All these signings are optional, but the signings of the hands and feet are even more optional, placed in brackets within brackets. However, these actions are very expressive and many parishes include them all. You sign the group afterward as you do near the end of Mass. I like to make a big sign of the cross, reaching high and dipping low. After all of this, there should be no doubt that following Christ means taking up his cross.

Everyone may sing or say an acclamation in praise of Christ. Try to avoid singing in praise of the candidates.

The only reference to your thumb is in 54, option A. Just as you sign infants with your thumb at the start of their baptism, so you sign adults in accepting them as catechumens. However, many parishes use a bigger gesture, one that respects the age of the person being signed and the hope of the assembly to see what's going on. So, for example, I open my hand and use its heel to make the sign of the cross on someone's forehead. I move my hand like a paintbrush, and I make an effort to touch the forehead with some pressure, so the person feels truly signed. I encourage sponsors and catechists to do the same. Some of them instinctively use the thumb or trace the sign of the cross in the air. But these symbols are not as expressive as a good hard signing. One bishop told me he uses his thumb*nail* to carve a cross in each candidate's forehead! I think that is too much, but the point is to seal this person with the cross of Christ. If you feel you must use your thumb, at least try to move your entire hand in the form of the cross. If you hold your hand in one place while making the cross with your thumb, very few people will see it. If you move your whole hand, more will grasp what you are doing.

Notice that the word "catechumens" appears for the first time after the last signations, as the group responds, "Amen." Candidates who accept the gospel and are signed with the cross change their status to catechumens.

57. A prayer concludes the signings. At Mass this prayer replaces the collect. Two options are offered. Incidentally, the Latin original of the first option has "*N. and N.*" after the word "catechumens." It's a good idea to use the names of the candidates as much as possible. It personalizes the liturgy and it helps everyone know who is who.

58. In rare circumstances, the catechumen may take a new name. This option was included because of some mission territories, where converts to pagan religions took a new name to signify their new allegiance. Some Catholic missionaries thought their people should be allowed to take a new name to show the same kind of allegiance to Christ. Ordinarily, we don't do this in our culture. But in unusual circumstances, your bishop may permit it. I think it only makes sense if the person is also legally changing his or her name, and wants to be called something else from this day forward.

59. The bishop may also permit the inclusion of additional rites, for example, the presentation of a cross or some other symbolic act. You probably don't need more symbols at this point, but if you do, you may request permission for one from your bishop. The cross symbolizes one's desire to follow Christ and the kind of conversion underway. But most people will understand this already. Some parishes give the catechumen a large cross to wear around the neck. It may be done, but a pectoral cross is traditionally something worn by bishops, not catechumens. Theoretically, you could give catechumens a symbol of membership in your parish: a photo directory, a Catholic school sweatshirt, a coffee mug with your logo—but this would trivialize an otherwise meaningful celebration. You don't want to do that.

If you present a cross, you say the text proposed in *RCIA* 74.

60. You invite the catechumens and sponsors to enter the church. You're actually inviting everyone in, but the text is specifically addressed to the catechumens. You are welcoming them to share at the table of God's word. This is a significant moment, especially if you have so far conducted the liturgy outdoors. You are now inviting the catechumens to cross the threshold of the church. Even if they've done it dozens of times already, this crossing is momentous because of who they now are, who they will be in the midst of this assembly, and what they will hear when they take their place. A text is suggested, but you can extend this invitation in your own words.

The words may be accompanied with "some gesture of invitation." I guess you arrange your hands and arms in a gesture that says "Walk this way." But other gestures could be made: Place a hymnal in the hands of the catechumens so they can join in the song; or take their coat and hang it up. Perhaps the most natural gesture is to have the sponsors grab their hand, put a hand on their shoulder, or place an arm around their waist, and walk them into the church.

A song may be sung. Psalm 34 is suggested with an apt refrain about the rewards of listening. Another possibility is to continue with more verses of the song you used at the beginning of the liturgy.

61. When everyone is in place and the music is over, you speak briefly to the catechumens. Choose your own words. Tell them about the dignity of God's word, which is proclaimed and heard in this church. You are setting the stage for the Liturgy of the Word, and you are reminding all the faithful how important it is to pay attention to the readings.

Note: You omit the penitential act, the Glory to God, and the collect of this Mass.

The rubric says the Lectionary or a Bible is carried in the procession and placed on the lectern where it may be incensed. The *RCIA* predates the 2002 revision of the *General Instruction of the Roman Missal* (*GIRM*), which says the *Book of the Gospels*, not the Lectionary, is carried in the entrance procession (120d, 172). In the original Latin, the *RCIA* calls more generically for "a book of sacred Scriptures" to be carried in procession and set down with honor. In Latin it doesn't say which book or where to set it down. Remember, the *RCIA* imagines that this ceremony takes place at a word service, in which case the *Book of the Gospels* might not be used. The Latin text seems to imply that a special procession of this book follows your brief instruction. If you are celebrating this at Sunday Mass, it makes sense if the deacon or reader carries the *Book of the Gospels* in the procession with you and everyone else, and then stands at the altar, holding the book aloft until the singing is over and you have made your remarks about the significance of the Word of God. The *Book of the Gospels* would be placed on the altar. But if the Lectionary is used, it would logically be placed on the ambo, because it will be needed right away. If you are using incense, you may incense the book. We usually don't incense a Lectionary, so the symbols hold together better if you reserve incense for the *Book of the Gospels*. But the rite lets you incense the Lectionary at the ambo if you want. Once these gestures are completed, all would be seated for the Liturgy of the Word.

This is all that remains of a more complicated ceremony found in the eighth-century *Gelasian Sacramentary* (34). Today's *RCIA* includes presentations of the creed and the Lord's Prayer, but the Gelasian also had a presentation of the Gospels. Four deacons, each carrying a volume of one of the four Gospels, entered from the sacristy with candles and incense. They placed the books on the corners of the altar. The priest explained why the books are important. A deacon read the opening verses of the first Gospel, and then the priest explained the symbol for Matthew: a human being. The second deacon read the opening of Mark's Gospel, and the priest explained the meaning of the lion. And so on with Luke and John, the ox and the eagle.

An independent version of this ritual almost made its way into the revised catechumenate. After the Second Vatican Council, the inclusion of this presentation was proposed but rejected, partly because it did not share the antiquity of the other presentations, and partly because it was thought more appropriate to present a Bible at the beginning of one's formation, not at the end.

A tinier vestige of the presentation of the book still appears in the baptism of infants, when you invite the group to move from the door of the church to the front, where they listen to the readings (*RBC* 80).

62. The Lectionary includes a lovely selection of readings for this liturgy. The citations that appear in the *RCIA* can be found in volume IV of the *Lectionary for Mass* (743). As a reminder, the *RCIA* envisions that you are celebrating this at a word service, not a Eucharist, so you are completely free to use these passages in that context.

However, if you are celebrating this rite at Mass, other rules apply. On Sundays during the seasons of Advent, Lent, and Easter, one reading may customarily be chosen from those proposed in the rite (*LM* 88). On an Ordinary Time Sunday, you may replace all the regular scriptures with the ones for the rite of acceptance. In practice, this is rarely done because of the appeal of the standard Sunday readings. But if you are struggling with the readings and you want to make the rite of acceptance a centerpiece, you may swap one or more of the texts.

63. You give a homily. Make it good. Connect the readings with the journey of the catechumens, and challenge people to live in a way that keeps striving toward the prize of eternal life.

64. A book containing the Gospels may be given to the catechumens. This is another variation of the impressive ritual from the *Gelasian Sacramentary*; see 61. The *RCIA* may confuse you about the nature of this book. The section bears the title "Presentation of a Bible." But the description is of "a book containing the Gospels." In Latin, it calls for a "little books of the Gospels," as if the catechumens are to receive pocketbook editions suitable for carrying around. This gift is optional.

If you give it, make it meaningful. For example, a catechist could be the one to give the book. You may still say, "Receive the Gospel of Jesus Christ, the Son of God," or something like that. Another variation is to have the catechist or deacon or reader hold the parish *Book of the Gospels*, especially if the rite takes place during Sunday Mass. He or she opens it to the Gospel of the day, and shows it to each catechumen. Meanwhile, the catechist or you may say something that recalls the earlier dialogue (51). For example, you could say, "Receive the Gospel of Jesus Christ, the source of our unity," "the giver of faith," "the healer of sadness," or whatever seems appropriate. Each catechumen responds, but the rubrics do not say how. It will probably look right if the catechumen kissed the book, as the priest or deacon does after proclaiming the sacred text. The catechumen could also touch the book, or respond with words such as, "Thanks be to God." Everyone could sing an acclamation. You have a lot of freedom here.

A cross may also be given, unless this happened earlier (59). But this part of the liturgy is focused on the word, so introducing a cross here will seem out of step.

65. Intercessions follow. The ones listed in the rite are suggestions. They may be rewritten or replaced with others. You may also use these intercessions for the prayer of the faithful for the Mass, adding to them some universal petitions. Separating these intercessions from the prayer of the faithful keeps the purpose of the intentions distinct. And, in fact, the prayer of the faithful is literally that: "of the *faithful*." It is to be made by all the baptized as part of their priestly office. But you may combine them. It gives a Sunday liturgy a better flow. You don't have to combine all the petitions from both sets. Just make up a list of average length that combines the essential elements of each.

66. You have two options for the closing prayer for the intercessions. Either one works. You stretch out your hands over the catechumens as you offer the prayer. In some parishes the assembly also extends hands as an exterior sign of their interior prayer. This assures the elect that everyone loves them, supports them, and prays for them as they approach baptism. Note that the first option encourages you to speak their names again. It is usually a good idea to repeat the names of the catechumens in public; see 57.

67. The catechumens may be dismissed. Some people find this horrifying. "We've just welcomed these catechumens, and now we're telling them to go away?" Well, yes.

In the early days of the church, catechumens were not allowed to stay for the Liturgy of the Eucharist. It was too easy to misunderstand what was going on, so church leaders wanted only catechized believers in there. Catechumens were warmly welcomed to take part in the Liturgy of the Word, and then sent out with a formal dismissal. For centuries, we used to call the two parts of the service "the Mass of the catechumens" and "the Mass of the faithful."

Nowadays, anyone can go to any Mass, or watch one on television. So the dismissal seems unwarranted. However, the option has been retained because it helps catechumens concentrate more intently on the word, and it reminds the faithful how privileged they are to stay.

In practice, many parishes have made this into a "dismissal to" rather than a "dismissal from." The catechumens are sent forth to continue their reflection. They talk about the readings and the homily. They receive catechesis about the Church. They go perform some action for justice. They grow in faith. So we dismiss them "to" a specific activity. But in the old days, they were honestly being dismissed "from" the Christian assembly, and made free to go home. The *RCIA* has the same possibility in mind.

If you are dismissing the catechumens, options A and B are presented for your choice. Use A if the catechumens are going home; use B if they are going to reflect more deeply on the scriptures. You may, of course, make up a formula of your own. Option C is a sample of what you say if the catechumens are not dismissed. But note that the rubrics say this is used "for serious reasons." Option D is for a word service, in which everyone will be dismissed at the same time. If using that option, all may sing a closing song.

If the catechumens are going into a session, a catechist may walk out with them as a sign of the church's concern, perhaps carrying the Lectionary or the *Book of the Gospels*; see p. 32.

68. If you celebrate this rite at Mass, the rest of the liturgy proceeds as usual. If you have incorporated the prayer of the faithful with the intercessions for the catechumens, go right to the creed. Or you may omit the creed on this occasion. But I think this is an especially fine occasion for the faithful remaining in the church to profess the faith that binds them, the faith these catechumens long to share. Wait until the catechumens have left—they do not own the creed until its presentation to them during Lent.

After the profession of faith, sit down immediately. People are expecting the prayer of the faithful. By sitting you will cue the ushers to start the collection, and the musicians to take up the song. You know how the rest of Mass goes.

Acceptance into the Order of Catechumens [for Children] (RCIA 262-276)

If a child of catechetical age is to be baptized, he or she should be accepted into the order of catechumens and prepared for full initiation at the Easter Vigil. These children would be about age 6 and older, the age of those who would typically be admitted to preparation for their first confession, confirmation, or First Communion.

In designing the postconciliar liturgy, the Catholic Church made a special outreach to children. The revised baptism of infants better takes their age into account. There is now a *Directory for Masses with Children*, a Lectionary and Eucharistic Prayers for them, as well as special texts for penance, anointing the sick, and funerals. The *RCIA* developed an entire section devoted to the initiation of children of catechetical age (252–329).

260. For the rite of acceptance the *RCIA* envisions a small congregation so that the children will not feel uncomfortable. To some American catechists and parents this seems an unnecessary accommodation. When questioned about it, German theologian Balthasar Fischer, who helped design these rites, famously remarked that German children were shy. (I'm sure there are German parents who would disagree.) Fischer had no problem inviting a larger assembly of the faithful to gather in support of children comfortable with the spotlight.

261. The rite is celebrated in church or some other place where children can "experience a warm welcome." That might be in the parish school, or some other location that feels like home to them. The church, though, is probably the best choice. As with the adult rite, this liturgy makes most sense if you begin outside and cross the threshold of the building as the prayer progresses.

According to the *RCIA* this service normally does not take place during Mass. It imagines that most of those attending would not be receiving Communion. For example, the child might be so young that his or her peers would only now be preparing for First Communion. Still, this rite may fruitfully take place at a parish Mass at school or on Sunday.

262. A priest or deacon presides wearing an alb or surplice with stole. This presumes that the rite does not include Mass. If you are leading the rite during Mass, wear a chasuble; see 48.

The children are supposed to be waiting "with their parents or guardians or, alternatively, with their sponsors." Paragraph 260 explains this: Parents or guardians are preferred. But if they cannot attend, sponsors may stand in their place. Eventually the children will need godparents, but at this stage their parents or guardians should present them if possible.

263. You *and the community* greet the children. Everyone tries to make the kids feel at home. The beginning is completely informal, but if you are starting Mass with this rite, you would logically make the sign of the cross and extend a liturgical greeting (e.g., "The Lord be with you"). You introduce the ceremony in your own words.

You invite the children and their parents (or sponsors) forward; see 260 and also 49. If the godparents have been selected and are present, they could stand up as well, but the rite does not expect this. The parents are preferred. Depending on the space, people may already be in place, and you may not need to have anyone step forward. Just use common sense.

264. You adapt the opening dialogue to the circumstances of the children. They may respond with simple statements. You might discuss this conversation with their catechist ahead of time and work out the phrasing you think will work best.

These questions differ from those in the adult rite (50). You ask the children, "What do you want to become?" and "Why?" These queries stem from the Ambrosian Catholic tradition, and they have been around for a long time. In drafts of the *RCIA*, they appeared as an alternate set of questions for adults. Before the book was published, though, they were arbitrarily shifted over to the version of this rite for children. They are good questions. They model the kind of conversation that should unfold between you and the youngsters.

You continue with a brief catechesis; see 52. As with the adults, you may link this to statements made in the preceding dialogue, child by child. I conduct the dialogue, invite the cross-bearer forward. Have the sponsor or parent place the child's hands on the cross, and then give the catechesis. I will improvise this, based on what I hear the child say. If the child has said he or she wants to be a friend of Jesus, I might say something about how Jesus spent a lot of time with his friends and asked them to be the kind of friends who helped out when he got into trouble. "Will you be a friend of Jesus even when it's hard?" Something like that.

The child should give some assent to this statement. The rubric suggests that the child repeat the last line of the catechesis: "Love God with all your heart and love one another as I have loved you." That might work, but it's a mouthful for a little kid. Any affirmative response will do. Even a nod of the head would suffice for the child's assent.

265. You gain the assent of the parents or sponsors and the entire assembly; see 53 and also 260. The text says you ask the children to bring their parents or sponsor forward. But they are already standing there, according to 263. You ask the parents or sponsor to give consent and to pledge their support. Then you ask everyone else if they will, too.

266. The signing with the cross takes place as it does for adults (54). It is recommended that the signing of the other senses be reserved for older children, but younger ones would probably benefit from this as well. You may decide case by case.

267. The signing of the forehead is similar to the adult version of this rite (55), but the words have been simplified, and a little more explanation is given.

268. The signing of the other senses is optional, and the hands and feet are even more optional (cf. 56). Notice that the words are simplified to help the children understand them.

According to the rubric, you may sign the other senses yourself, but be prudent. Some parents may prefer to perform these actions themselves.

The adult version of the rite includes a prayer and an optional presentation of a cross (57 and 59). These are omitted in the rite for children. No explanation for these omissions is given. The intent may be to keep things simple.

269. You invite the group to enter the church or wherever it is that the celebration is taking place; see 261 and 60. The church makes the best choice for a point of destination. It is expected that the children may have peers who are baptized Catholic. The new catechumens join that group to show they are now part of its assembly. A song may be sung. The psalms recommended (95 and 122) are about listening to God and joyfully entering God's house.

You may extend this invitation with the words in the book, or use your own words. No gesture is suggested (cf. 60). But whatever you do or say, it should be obvious to the children that they are welcome inside.

270. You give a brief instruction on the Liturgy of the Word (cf. 61). Keep it simple, so the children can understand you.

As in the adult rite, you may have the Lectionary, Bible, or *Book of the Gospels* carried in procession, set on the ambo, and incensed. See the remarks on p. 21.

271. The readings may be those recommended for adults (cf. 62), but you are free to choose other texts. If the children have been using some scripture texts in their preparation thus far, you may use those at this time.

If you are celebrating this on a day when ritual Mass texts cannot be used—such as a Sunday in Advent, Lent, or Easter—you may substitute only one reading (*LM* 88).

272. You give a homily; see 63. The rite suggests a brief one. Then you invite the children to silent prayer. They are capable of this, and it is good for them to learn this skill during catechesis, and even at home.

A song may be sung after the homily. This recommendation appears in the *Directory for Masses with Children* (46). It is one way that children can respond to the Liturgy of the Word.

273. As an option, the children may receive a book containing the Gospels (cf. 64). They may receive this during or after the song. Somehow, someone has explained this to them, or explains it now. You are free to include this or omit it.

274. The intercessions follow. The specific intentions in the rite are suggestions. If you like them, use them. If not, you may write your own. As in the rite for adults (65), if this takes place at Mass these may be combined with the prayer of the faithful.

275. Extend your hands over the catechumens as you pray for them. The adult rite gives you two options for this prayer (66), but only one is supplied for children. In some parishes the entire community extends its hands. See comments on p. 24.

276. You dismiss the people, and everyone sings a song. That ends the celebration, unless you continue with Mass. In that case, only the children who are catechumens are dismissed, and the Mass continues as usual (cf. 67).

If you have both adults and children to be accepted into the order of catechumens, you have a decision to make. You may celebrate these rites separately for the two groups. Or you may combine them, making adjustments where you see fit. The *RCIA* suggests this approach when both children and adults celebrate the rite of election (279).

Whether you celebrate this rite with adults or with children, you or the catechist should have a conversation afterward with the new catechumens. Talk about the ceremony, what they were experiencing, and how they feel now. Immediately after the celebration you could offer some kind of reception. The people from your parish who participated in the rite might enjoy the chance to say a few words of encouragement to the catechumens in a social setting.

Dismissals
(RCIA 67)

At a typical Sunday Mass you are to dismiss catechumens kindly after the Liturgy of the Word (*RCIA* 75/3). If their dismissal presents "practical or pastoral problems," they may stay. However, they are not yet baptized members of the faithful, part of God's priestly people. It is the baptized who profess their creed, offer the prayer of the faithful, join in the offering, sing their parts of the Eucharistic Prayer, say the prayer Jesus taught his disciples, and who share in Communion. Catechumens are dismissed not just because they are not yet eligible for Communion, but because they are not yet eligible to fulfill the tasks expected of all the faithful throughout the second part of the Mass.

The Liturgy of the Word, though, is open to all, because through the word God instructs those who hear. The catechumens belong with the assembly of the faithful for the first part of Mass.

67. Sample formulas for dismissal appear at the end of the rite of acceptance and elsewhere in the book. You may improvise on these, drawing out a theme from the readings or from your homily.

In many communities, a catechist also leaves with the catechumens. He or she may carry the Lectionary or the *Book of the Gospels* as a sign that Sunday's word will continue to form the group. This works best if the catechist has already participated at Mass or will do so later that Sunday. It is hard to convince catechumens of the centrality of the Sunday Eucharist if their own catechist does not share Communion that day. In situations where the catechist cannot participate in another Mass, he or she should probably remain for the Liturgy of the Eucharist while the catechumens get started on their own. The catechist can take up the session after Mass.

You may add a minor exorcism or blessing to the dismissal (81, 83/2, 89). The *RCIA* includes a collection of these among the rites belonging to the period of the catechumenate. These prayers may be offered during a word service apart from Mass, but the Liturgy of the Word *at Mass* may be the "rite" in which the catechumens participate on any given Sunday (81, second option).

Minor exorcisms may be given by a priest, deacon, or catechist appointed for this responsibility by the bishop (91). They draw attention to the struggle between flesh and spirit, the importance of self-denial, and one's unending need of God's help (90).

You may conduct a minor exorcism during Sunday Mass after the homily. You invite the catechumens forward. A catechist may step up to the ambo, pick up the Lectionary or *Book of the Gospels*, elevate it slightly, and stand someplace central. The catechumens bow or kneel, and you extend your hands over the group while you offer one of the prayers (94). Choose one you think fits the circumstances: Some refer to familiar scripture passages (D, F, G, H, and I, for example). Others are more generic in their design. Any one of these should comfort the catechumens with the assurance that all are looking after their needs.

After the prayer, the catechumens lift their heads or stand up, and you dismiss them with kind words. The catechist may lead them out, carrying the word of God.

The blessings follow a similar structure (95–97). These are signs of God's love and the Church's care (95). As with the minor exorcisms, a blessing may be given by a priest, deacon, or catechist appointed by the bishop (96).

After the homily and a period of silence, the catechumens come forward. They do not bow their heads or kneel—this will be a blessing, not an exorcism. You extend your hands over the group while you say the prayer. Or you say the prayer and have the catechumens come to you one by one; in that case you impose hands on each one's head. They then depart. A catechist could take part in this (16). Sponsors might accompany the catechumens.

You may pray a minor exorcism or a blessing on any occasion that you dismiss catechumens from the liturgy. Or you may have a dismissal without one by simply inviting the group to go forth.

85–89. If you would like to use these apart from Mass, visit a catechetical session, or invite the group to meet you at church some time. Pray with them briefly in a celebration of the word that concludes with an exorcism or blessing.

You may anoint catechumens privately, normally during a word service (100). Use the oil of catechumens, the same oil you may use just before baptizing infants. The bishop blesses it at the Mass of chrism each year. If you run out, you are permitted to bless more yourself (101). Use any vegetable oil, but olive oil is traditional. Don't add perfume—that's the recipe for chrism, and only a bishop can consecrate that.

You may anoint catechumens more than one time (100). The ceremony should take place during the period of the catechumenate; that is, between the rite of acceptance and the rite of election. Incidentally, the practice of anointing catechumens is quite ancient in the Church, but the *occasion* for this anointing is new. Formerly, anointings all took place during the immediate preparation for baptism, during the weeks just before Easter. They accompanied the major exorcisms of the scrutinies; see *RBC* 49–50. But the framers of the revised catechumenate felt that the season of Lent was getting crowded with rituals. So the anointing was moved to a position earlier in the process. It is easy to overlook this ceremony, but it is good to include it.

Think of the anointing as a seal on the prayers of exorcism. You are praying that the catechumens will have strength in their spiritual struggles, and that all evil temptations will be kept away (99). The oil of catechumens is like sunscreen or bug spray. It is supposed to protect them when they go out into the world.

Only a priest or deacon may anoint with the oil of catechumens (98). Even where priests are so scarce that some lay catechists are deputed to baptize infants, catechists are not to use the oil of catechumens. Only priests and deacons do.

102. The anointing takes place after the homily. It may be done at a Sunday Mass. Invite the catechumens forward. Say a prayer. Two options are given. One is a prayer over the catechumens. It is identical to minor exorcism 94 H. You may replace this with any other minor exorcism from *RCIA* 94. The other option is a prayer over the oil. Use the first option if you have oil blessed by the bishop; use the second if you need to bless oil before the anointing.

103. You recite the formula for anointing, and then anoint each catechumen on the breast, on both hands, or on other parts of the body. By "breast" it probably means the sternum. The ancient texts speak of anointing catechumens "between the shoulders"—probably in front of the body at the neck. If it is difficult to anoint this area with decorum, you may safely choose to anoint hands.

You may conclude with a prayer of blessing (cf. 97). This ceremony evokes the drama of the spiritual life by its subtle use of prayers and signs.

Members of the assembly will be better able to participate in this ritual if the catechumens stand in the sanctuary facing them, not the altar. They will also better see what you are doing when you anoint.

Welcoming the Candidates (RCIA 416–433)

When you have uncatechized, baptized Christians who want to join the Catholic Church, you may celebrate with them a rite of welcoming to mark the beginning of their formation. The same rite may be used with baptized Catholic adults who received little or no religious education or the sacraments of confirmation and First Communion, but who now seek a more active role in the Church. The ceremony is parallel to the rite of acceptance into the order of catechumens and is based upon its words and signs; see 48.

The rubrics never indicate that a deacon may preside, but he is eligible to do so for the rite of acceptance and for the combined rite; see 48 and 507. Certainly if this takes place during Mass, the priest should preside.

Be a good priest for these Christians. Get to know them and their spiritual journey; learn who the sponsors are. Be sure that someone has spent enough time with them to discern their readiness for this celebration, and help them prepare their responses to the questions they will hear during the rite. Rehearse the sponsors. You may celebrate this rite more than once a year, preferably at a Mass when no other special celebration is taking place.

This rite is optional. Many people like it because it allows baptized Christians to make a public statement about their hunger for other sacraments, and because it gives parish members the names and faces of those who are seeking a closer relationship with them. And, after all, it's called a rite of welcoming. Who could be against welcoming?

Well, me. I am not a big fan of this rite, but I do use it from time to time. It was designed for those who have little or no experience in Christianity (Appendix III: National Statutes for the Catechumenate [NS] 31). Many baptized Christians expressing a desire to become Catholic already have lived the faith they have received, know the Bible well, and have a close relationship with Christ. This rite was not designed for them. But many parishes are putting them through it anyway. For those who are already baptized, the path to the table should be as direct as possible. The rite of welcoming is for uncatechized Christians, it is optional, and in many cases it is advisable to omit it.

You may include baptized Christian children of catechetical age, though the *RCIA* never says what to do about them. If they were baptized *Catholic*, there is no need for this rite because they will prepare for confirmation and First Communion with their peers. But if they were baptized in another Christian church, you could use this rite. The only problem is that it was designed for baptized and previously uncatechized adults (411); that is, for people who never had or never took the opportunity for catechesis. Children of catechetical age are uncatechized for a different reason: they are children. Their situation does not differ that much from their Catholic peers.

Even though I like to avoid this rite, you may use it. And if you do, here are some things to note:

416. The *RCIA* presumes that you are celebrating this rite in the context of Mass. These candidates are among the faithful; they cannot become catechumens. So they have a place with baptized Catholics when the Church gathers for Eucharist.

Note that the candidates are to be seated in a prominent place among the faithful. If they were unbaptized, going through the rite of acceptance, they would preferably start this liturgy outside; see 48. But this rite wants them indoors, in an honored place among the faithful with whom they share baptism.

Mass begins with the entrance song as usual. You process in as usual. You may be tempted to include the candidates in the entrance procession, but they are seated among the faithful to show how similar they are, not how different they are.

417. You greet everyone and introduce the ceremony; see 49. The rite doesn't say when you do this, but it makes sense to do it after the sign of the cross and the greeting (e.g., "The Lord be with you.") The opening dialogue (418) may replace the penitential act and the Glory to God.

As in the parallel rite for the unbaptized, you may say a little about these candidates. But I usually have a sponsor do it later on.

You invite the candidates and sponsors forward. Musicians may sing something, and Psalm 63 is recommended. But if the movement only takes a moment, you may not need more music. It is doubtful you will use all eight recommended verses of this psalm.

I usually ask the sponsor to guide the candidate forward, hand on shoulder. I have the sponsors and candidates turn and face the people.

418. You conduct the opening dialogue; see 50. Two options are given, but "similar words may be used." In one option, you ask the candidate to state his or her name. If there are many candidates, you may ask once and have them each respond. Alternatively, you may call out the names of the candidates, and they say they are present.

I prefer a variation in which I introduce the sponsor, and then ask him or her to introduce the candidate. In this case, the sponsor takes over part of your introduction to the service. This establishes the sponsor's role of helping the candidates meet the community and learning about its way of life.

Then you talk to each of the candidates. You may ask the question suggested in the book, "What do you ask of God's Church?", or you may ask their intentions some other way.

A suggested response is also given, but candidates should be able to answer this in their own words. This response can be profound, and it will be if someone rehearses with the candidates in the days before the ceremony. What *are* they asking of God's Church? More meaning in their life? A sense of belonging to something and some One? A better set of values than those they've followed so far? A family gathered at God's table as well as the table at home? Candidates should be able to put words onto their wishes, and we the Church gathered around need to hear about their expectations of us.

The candidate's suggested response appears in two forms. The first one mentions confirmation and Eucharist, whereas the second (in parentheses) speaks only of reception into the full communion of the Catholic Church. Most likely, the first version is designed for baptized Catholics who never received catechesis for any other sacrament. The second response is for other baptized Christians now joining the Catholic Church. Both responses are merely suggestions.

419. You ascertain the candidates' declaration of intent. They have just told you *what* they want. Now you ask them *why* they want it. The rite offers two versions of this.

In the first you say something about God's goodness, and then ask the candidates if they will join the community in its life of prayer and service. Notice the wording here. It affirms their desire to "continue" a journey of faith. This rite presumes that the candidates have already been on the journey—however rich or imperfect—with Christ as their companion.

In the second option, you invite the candidates to explain their desire in their own words. This has the advantage of letting the community hear from each candidate why he or she seeks formation for the sacraments. The personal testimony can take any shape, but it works best if it says something about how they got interested in the Catholic sacraments, and what they hope will happen as a result of sharing them.

When unbaptized candidates engage in the parallel rite, I involve the cross-bearer as part of this conversation (cf. 52). The candidates are taking up the gospel for the first time. But here, the baptized have already met Christ at some level. Some parishes use the cross image in the same way for baptized candidates as they do for unbaptized catechumens. You may. The rite allows this flexibility. But another way to help distinguish the dignity of the baptized is not to have them grasp the cross during the conversation. They are already following Christ.

420. You ask the sponsors and the rest of the assembly for their support; see 53. The rite suggests you address the entire group with one question. However, because you may use these or similar words, I usually ask the sponsors first, receive their response, and then question the community. It cues the sponsors about their special role, and it alerts all the people that we need their help too.

You say a prayer—actually an acclamation of praise for what God is doing. Your text ends with a sentence that everyone is supposed to repeat: "We praise you, Lord, and we bless you." People will not spontaneously know what to say. Prepare a printed sheet for them, or have a cantor or reader help with the response. I usually recite the first part of the prayer, and then sing the last line. People are apt to repeat the words and the notes after me.

421. You sign the candidates with the cross. You may sign only the forehead, or you may add more parts of the body—the same options given in the rite of acceptance for unbaptized candidates; see 54–55. Personally, I like limiting this to the forehead. The signing of all the senses is very expressive, and many baptized candidates and sponsors have responded favorably to experiencing it. But we need more ways to make this rite different from the rite of acceptance, and I think this is one way it can be done.

422. The forehead of the candidates is actually signed by their sponsors or catechists. You make the sign of the cross over the entire group, and sponsors or catechists trace the cross on the forehead.

I usually invite the sponsors or catechists to make a big gesture here, open their hand, and trace the cross on the forehead with the heel of the hand, while applying some pressure. The signing should be visible by those in attendance and felt by those being signed.

Notice that your lines say they are receiving the cross as a reminder of their baptism. You do not say, "Learn to know and follow Christ," as you do in the case of those who are unbaptized (55). The presumption is that they already belong to Christ and do not need to be claimed for him, and that the cross will remind them of their baptism.

All sing an acclamation. Some published musical versions of this acclamation have the congregation singing some words of support to the candidates, but the text more aptly suggests an acclamation of praise to Christ.

You may have the sponsors or catechists sign the other senses while you recite the appropriate texts. After each one, the people may sing an acclamation in praise of Christ.

When this is completed, you may make the sign of the cross over the whole group once, or over each one individually, as you do at the end of Mass. You recite the appropriate text.

424. You say the collect of the Mass; see 57. This may be the one given here, or it may be the one for the Mass of the day. If this is a Sunday in Advent, Lent, or Easter, or some other day of great importance, use the prayer of the day. But on a Sunday in Ordinary Time, it makes perfect sense to use this one.

There is no suggestion you present baptized candidates with a physical cross to keep, or that you conduct some other symbolic act. They do not take a new name. They already have the name with which they were baptized; see 58–59. Nor do you invite them to enter the church, as you would do for an unbaptized catechumen (60). This ritual has begun in the church, so there is no need to enter it, and baptized candidates should not be confused with the unbaptized, who symbolically cross a threshold.

425. You speak to the candidates and sponsors, explaining the dignity of God's word. This instruction is borrowed from the rite for the unbaptized (61), so it presumes that your candidates have little or no familiarity with the importance of a Bible. In fact, because the instructions have you address the *sponsors* as well, it presumes rather callously they are also in the dark. If you are doing this with people who know about the Bible, be careful what you say.

The rite does not call for the ceremonial enthronement and incensation of the book, as happens in the rite of acceptance for catechumens (61).

426. The readings of the day should normally be used. But if the ones seem not to fit very well, you may substitute some others. However, if you are celebrating this at a Sunday Mass, theoretically you may switch one or more of the readings to something more appropriate, as you could do for the rite of acceptance (62). It's usually best to follow the order of scriptures given in the Lectionary for that Sunday. It keeps the big picture in place, and it reminds the candidates that the Church's official liturgy is something they let shape their lives.

427. Your homily explains the readings, but it may also explain the significance of this celebration. If you are celebrating this on a Sunday when you are preaching at some other Masses, you will probably use the homily you've already prepared, or make some adjustments to the text to acknowledge the presence of the candidates; see 63.

428. You may give the candidates a book containing the Gospels. You may say a text, such as, "Receive the Gospel of Jesus Christ, the Son of God." The candidates may respond in any appropriate way.

This presentation is optional, as it is for catechumens (64). It makes sense if your candidates have had little or no experience of the Bible.

Some parishes have used other variations on this presentation. For example, a catechist may present the parish's *Book of the Gospels* to each candidate. He or she opens the book and says something that calls to mind that candidate's statements from the dialogue in the first part of the Mass.

You can still say your line, and the candidate may kiss the book, touch it, say "Thanks be to God," or make some other appropriate response.

429. You continue Mass with the creed. Notice that no dismissal is called for; see 67. It is presumed that those who are baptized have a place within the gathering of the Christian faithful. Many candidates come from Churches that share this same creed. They recite it along with everyone else.

430. The general intercessions should include petitions on behalf of the candidates. There should only be one set of petitions. The rite of acceptance for catechumens allows two distinct sets of petitions—one before the dismissal, which is focused on the needs of the catechumens, and one afterward, which takes up the concerns for the Church and the world (65). But here, the candidates are part of the baptized faithful, and they participate in the prayer "of the faithful." You may amplify those prayers with one or more of the petitions from the *RCIA*. Or you may freely adapt them.

These prayers are based on those for catechumens. They have been lightly retouched to fit the situation of those already baptized.

431. You bring these intercessions to a close with a prayer. You stretch your hands out over the group of candidates; see 66.

432. If all this has taken place in a word service, everyone is dismissed together. All may sing a song, and the service concludes.

433. But if it is at Mass, keep going with the rest of it. You know what to do.

> ## Celebration of the Rite of Acceptance into the Order of Catechumens and of the Rite of Welcoming Baptized but Previously Uncatechized Adults Who Are Preparing for Confirmation and/or Eucharist or Reception into the Full Communion of the Catholic Church
> ## (RCIA 507–529)

If you want to have one celebration for candidates and catechumens beginning their formation, this combined rite was composed to help you. Although a deacon may preside for this combined rite, he would probably not do so if it takes place within Mass.

I don't like this rite at all, and I don't recommend using it. But it is in the *RCIA*, and you certainly may. I have used it on occasion more out of necessity than design. We've had some situations where it was proving impractical to separate the groups of baptized and unbaptized inquirers beginning their formation. But even when I use this combined rite, I exercise a number of options.

Once again, the rite of welcoming baptized candidates is optional. It does not need to be celebrated at all. If you cannot arrange separate weekends or separate Masses the same weekend to celebrate the rites of acceptance and welcoming distinctly, you still have the option of omitting the rite of welcoming. But do the rite of acceptance. It is an important step in the life of a catechumen; see p. 10.

The first thing I don't like about this rite is its title. Look at that. Any rite needing that many words in its *title* is already in trouble by trying to explain itself. But it is what it is.

507. You gather both groups outside the church. This sadly eliminates one of the chief differences the liturgy makes between catechumens and candidates. Candidates should begin the rite of welcoming inside the church in honored places, but in the combined rite, they yield to simplicity; see 48 and 416.

If the congregation has already assembled in the church, you or the cantor or the catechist or someone may invite them to go outside. This could happen before the opening song or after the greeting.

If this is taking place apart from the Mass, you wear a stole over an alb or a surplice; the cope is optional. Although this paragraph does not mention it, you would wear the chasuble if you are beginning Mass. All may sing a song.

If this is Mass, you should probably make the sign of the cross and give the greeting. Even outside of Mass, start with the greeting. The rubrics do not indicate this, but it is the logical way to begin.

508. You introduce the ceremony. You may tell everyone about the particular spiritual journeys of the candidates, but I usually let a sponsor do this later. The proceedings are so complex that the *RCIA* gives you a suggested text. This was not deemed necessary in the other versions of this rite (49 and 417).

You invite the sponsors and candidates forward, and music may be sung, for example Psalm 63. In reality, these people may already be in place, and music may not be necessary.

509. The opening dialogue is a combination of 50 and 418. But see 264 for another version of this for children. The only difference is that the candidates have a second question asking for a fuller response.

To me, the questions are not unique enough to separate the nature of the two groups. You may want to separate them spatially—candidates in one place, catechumens in another. Something should be done to indicate that candidates are already among the baptized, and those to become catechumens are not.

510. With your bishop's permission you may replace the first acceptance of the Gospel with the rite of exorcism and renunciation of false worship, but normally you will not do this. See the comments on 72, p. 16.

511. The combined rite envisions that you will ask the catechumens as a group for their acceptance of the gospel. I prefer to integrate this question into the previous piece. I ask it individually of each person after hearing what they are seeking. See the comments on 52, p. 17.

512. Similarly, I prefer to integrate the candidates' declaration of intent with the questions I've just asked. So, after asking each candidate what they are seeking and what this formation offers them, I add the next question to ascertain their willingness to engage in their formation. See the comments on 419, p. 39.

513. You ask the sponsors and the assembly to affirm their willingness to help the candidates follow Christ. This paragraph has you asking the entire group as a whole. But you could divide up the questions: one to the sponsors of those to become catechumens, another to the sponsors of the baptized candidates, and a third for the entire assembly.

Then you say or sing a prayer, and everyone responds with an acclamation. See the comments on 53 and 420, p. 18 and p. 39.

514–520. For the signations, you are to sign the forehead of the catechumens, then you oversee the signing of the other senses, then you sign the forehead of the candidates, and then oversee the signing of *their* other senses. I find this too repetitive, though it is good to separate the groups in some way. I would probably sign the foreheads consecutively, saying something that distinguishes those receiving a sign of their new life (515) from those receiving a sign of the life they already possess (518). Then I would have the sponsors of those becoming catechumens continue with the other signations, while not signing the other body parts of the baptized candidates. You are free to make some adjustments here. The point is to distinguish these groups without belaboring the liturgy. See the comments on 54–57 and 421–424, p. 18 and p. 40.

The combined rite makes no mention of having the catechumens take a new name or giving them a cross; see 58, 59, and 74. Normally in the United States the catechumens do not take a new name. If you want to give them a cross, you may. It will distinguish the groups again. But it shouldn't be necessary after all the ritual signing.

521. You invite both groups to the word of God. This invitation exists in the rite of becoming a catechumen (60), but not in the rite of welcoming the candidates. The former rite begins outdoors; the latter does not. The combined rite is to begin outside, so you have to invite people in. But I find this an unfortunate situation for the candidates, especially if you have mistakenly invited those who have already been nurtured by the Bible Sunday by Sunday and know the value of the word of God from personal experience. It's one of the reasons to avoid the combined rite. The candidates are treated here as if they are not baptized.

522. You give an instruction about the dignity of God's word. This combines 61 and 425. But remember, the rite of welcoming is not for baptized Christians who have some experience in the faith (National Statutes 31). This invitation places the baptized candidates in an awkward situation if they have already been nurtured by the word.

523. The recommended readings are those for catechumens (62). They really do not apply to the candidates. Abraham is founding a new chosen people. The psalm celebrates those chosen to be God's own. The Gospel is about discovering Jesus as the Messiah. Candidates should have moved beyond these texts already. But they are still suggested for the combined rite. Another option is to choose the readings of the day.

524. Your homily should help sort out what is going on, and how God's Spirit is active with each group.

525. You may present a book containing the Gospels. See the comments on 64 and 428, p. 23 and p. 41. Regarding baptized candidates, this ritual was designed for those unfamiliar with the Bible. If they have already been formed by it, this ritual is not for them. Catechumens may also have some experience of the Bible, but they are still using it as a guidebook toward baptism, which is a different exploration than the one taken up by the baptized, who are deepening their life in Christ.

526. The intercessions are exactly the same as those for catechumens (67), except for the last one, which adopts wording from the intercessions for candidates (430). Once again, for my tastes, the combining of the two groups in one liturgy leaves something to be desired. You may combine the regular parish intentions with all or some of these petitions.

527. The concluding prayer has been adjusted to include both groups.

528. You dismiss the catechumens, but there is no suggestion that baptized candidates be dismissed from Mass (see 67). I think this helps make the distinction clear. But if this takes place at a word service, all are dismissed together (D). A song may conclude the celebration.

529. The Liturgy of the Eucharist continues if this rite takes place at Mass. You are permitted to have the prayers of the faithful after the dismissal. Normally I think it is not necessary to separate the first group of intentions (526) from the second (529). But with a combined rite, if you are dismissing only the catechumens, you could make a case for having a second set of petitions. After the dismissal, all recite the creed, including the candidates. Then all would offer the parish's prayer of the faithful together before continuing with the Eucharist. It is a long Mass, and this may be too much to ask, but it just may make some sense.

If this takes place at a Sunday Mass and you combine the parish's petitions with the intercessions in 526, you will go from the creed directly into the collection. You might need to cue the ushers and musicians ahead of time so they know what's up (see 68 and 433).

By the way, some parishes like to have the baptized candidates carry the gifts up in procession. You may, but it always seems a little rude to me—as though you are inviting your neighbors to bring food for a dinner you're having with other friends, and then sending your neighbors home without letting them eat any of it.

Rite of Sending
(RCIA 111-117)

The rite of sending was created by the Church in the United States so that parishes could celebrate some form of the rite of election. In the history of the catechumenate, the principal rites all took place at the cathedral, where the bishop presided for all of them, including baptism. When the catechumenate was revised after the Second Vatican Council, the rites were redrafted for parish usage—except for the rite of election, which is conceived as a cathedral liturgy. It may take place in a parish (127, 279) if the bishop comes there or has delegated a priest there to lead it. But normally, this is a diocesan ceremony that retains some connection between the bishop and the initiates.

But the decision also meant that the second major step of the catechumenate (the first being the rite of acceptance) would take place away from the home parish, out of view of the community that had been supporting the catechumens by prayer and example. So, a rite for parishes was invented in the United States. It has the approval of the Vatican, but it does not exist in most other countries.

The key symbol of the rite of election is the signing of the book of the elect. During the ceremony the godparents give testimony about the catechumens, the bishop receives their witness and declares that the catechumens are now "elect"—that is, they are to be numbered among the new chosen people of God. Just as God chose a personal nation through the covenant with Abraham, so God is choosing a personal people through the covenant of baptism. By entering their names, the catechumens state their intention to complete their formation, and the book becomes a symbol of God's call.

The *RCIA* offers alternative occasions when the catechumens sign their name. This may take place either in the parish or at the cathedral. Arguments can be made either way. The decision is usually made on a diocesan level. I prefer having the signatures made at the cathedral liturgy because it lends more integrity to the rite of election. But the other way is acceptable. Just remember, if your catechumens are signing their names at the rite of sending in your parish, that does not make them "elect." They become elect when the bishop declares them so. The rite of sending is just that—a preliminary ritual exercised by the parish so that more people grasp the significance of the cathedral ceremony.

The rite is optional. You do not have to use it at all, but it helps the parish follow the spiritual journey of their catechumens, and it helps the catechumens prepare for the rite of election.

Note that this rite is for the *unbaptized*. There is a parallel optional rite for baptized candidates (p. 54) and a combined rite for both groups (p. 59).

Some discernment should take place beforehand. Catechumens should become elect only after some real discussion about their progress. They don't advance to the final stage of preparation just because everyone else in the group is going forward, or because it's that time of year. You and the catechumenate team must judge their readiness (119, 121, and 122), and determine if they have undergone a conversion in mind and action, and acquired a good understanding of Christian teaching as well as a spirit of faith and charity (120).

Before the rite of acceptance, a similar discernment took place; see p. 11. Now a more thorough determination is to be made. The last six weeks of preparation are a time for spiritual formation, not for cramming dogmas. The decision that someone is ready for baptism is made prior to the rite of election. All that's left is for them to prepare their minds and spirits for the sacraments of initiation.

Practically speaking, that means any annulments and convalidations should probably be resolved prior to this time. The rite of election declares that there are no more obstacles to baptism. You don't want any surprises to come up in the last few weeks.

111. This ceremony may take place during a word service (109), but many parishes integrate it into a Sunday Mass. It should happen shortly before the rite of election—either the previous weekend or earlier in the day. The sending begins after the homily.

The homily appropriately includes an explanation and exhortation about divine election. There are other ways to frame the meaning of the rite and to evoke a response from it, but the homily presents a unique opportunity. However you do it, I think the homily should be an integrated whole, not a series of disconnected ideas, and that the entire liturgy should not belabor the point of the ritual. Give the homily some thought and preparation. This event signifies a major step for the elect and the community. Make it memorable.

Someone presents the catechumens and explains the ceremony. In most churches, this person will need a microphone. Avoid having him or her use the ambo if at all possible. That piece of furniture should be reserved for the readings, the homily, and the prayers of the faithful. If you have a wireless mic, a lectern, or a cantor stand with a secondary microphone, use it.

The rubrics never indicate that this speaker is introduced, but it would be polite if you told everyone who it is and why she or he is speaking. For example, "I'd like to introduce N., the director of our catechumenate, who will begin today's ceremony." Or the speaker could say, "Good morning, everyone. I'm N., and it's been my privilege to work with those people from our community who are preparing for baptism this Easter." Something like that.

Notice that this ceremony involves godparents, not sponsors. For the difference, see 10 and 11. The framers of the revised catechumenate thought up the idea of separating the two roles. They thought that the parish might supply a sponsor to help catechumens through their time of preparation, and that the catechumen might select a different person as godparent for the final few weeks. I'm not sure this was a great idea. It contributes to the notion that the godparent hasn't been involved in the spiritual formation of the catechumen and is coming in for ceremonial duties only. The sponsor and the godparent may be the same person, but they may be separate, and some catechumens may actually prefer it.

After the introduction, you invite the catechumens forward with their godparents. They are called by name, but the ritual does not specify who calls them. It's probably easier if the one who made the introduction continues with this responsibility. Or a deacon could extend the invitation since he is traditionally the one who invites the assembly to perform changes of posture and position.

When they get into place, the catechumens don't need to say anything, but the godparents do. You may want to station them where a microphone can pick up their words. The rubric says they are to stand "before the celebrant," but this ceremony works better if more people can see the faces of the catechumens. It depends on the arrangement of your church, but you may have the godparents lead the catechumens into the sanctuary, turn them to face the assembly, and stand behind them, hand on the shoulder as a sign of support. Godparents can either speak from there or step forward to a microphone when it is their turn.

112. You give a brief explanation of what everyone needs to do: accept the responsibility to inquire about the readiness of the catechumens.

You ask the godparents a series of questions about the catechumens' attitude, example, and readiness. The godparents answer these questions in the affirmative. This will have integrity if the discernment has happened earlier. Then this conversation is simply a summary of a process that has been going on for some time.

As an alternative, some parishes ask the godparents to give a personal testimony in place of the questions and answers. In this event, the godparent would step to the microphone and explain how the catechumen has demonstrated readiness for initiation. It will usually go better if someone rehearses the godparents ahead of time. They may write out their remarks to keep themselves focused. But when they speak, it should sound sincere.

The rubrics permit the entire assembly to express its approval of the catechumens. This could happen in different ways. If the godparent has given personal testimony about a catechumen's progress in faith, you may ask if anyone else in the community has something to add. It depends on the nature of your community and the structure of your church, but this can be a very life-giving exercise. You could open the floor after each godparent has spoken, or after all godparents have spoken. People may then spontaneously give live testimony.

Alternatively, you could ask the assembly a ritual question, such as, "Do you agree with the testimony of the godparent?" They all would answer, "Yes," or "We do."

I like to do it this way: Everyone is seated, and a godparent gives testimony about catechumen X. Then I turn to the assembly and say, "Would those of you who know catechumen X please stand?" Then I ask that group the question: "Do you agree with the testimony of the godparent?" I do the same for catechumens Y and Z. The idea is to lend integrity to this dialogue. People who don't know the catechumens have no business testifying to their readiness. And those people who don't know catechumens X, Y, or Z may ask themselves why they never took the effort to meet these people during their period of formation.

Another way to ask everyone to express approval of the candidates is to cue their applause. For example, you could say something such as this: "N., N., *and* N., your godparents have spoken favorably about you, and we all want to assure you of our prayers and support. Congratulations on the spiritual progress you have made." I avoid saying, "Let's give them a hand." The applause seems more sincere if people spontaneously react to words of congratulations.

You affirm the testimony and declare that the catechumens are being recommended to the bishop, who will call them to initiation. Notice that you do not name them among the elect. That is for the bishop or his delegate to do.

113. If catechumens sign the book of the elect at the cathedral, they do not sign it here. But if you are to present signatures that will be assembled into the book at the cathedral, then they should be made now. Catechumens are permitted to sign their names after the celebration on some other occasion prior to the rite of election, but it is difficult to know why anyone would do that. If the names are not to be signed in the presence of the bishop, get it done in this ceremony.

RCIA 123 says that godparents may sign their names together with the catechumens. It is optional. An antecedent for this practice appears in the homilies of Theodore of Mopsuestia (+428), in which a minister inscribed the names of both catechumens and godparents at the start of Lent. However, the English rendering of *RCIA* 123 appears to be an overtranslation of the Latin, which simply states that the godparents may inscribe "the name" with the catechumens. It refers to the rubric in *RCIA* 132, which allows a godparent or a minister to inscribe the names *of the catechumens*. In Latin the rubrics never clearly state that the godparents may sign their own names. The approved English translation permits it, but very few places practice it, probably because it confuses the point of signing the book.

The rite of sending has no other instruction concerning the signing of the names. When names are signed in the rite of election, a song such as Psalm 16 or Psalm 33 may be sung, with a refrain about being chosen by God (132). If names are to be signed during the rite of sending, catechumens may inscribe their own names, or they may call out their names and have the godparents or someone else sign. But this ceremony has more significance if the catechumens sign their own names.

114. Intercessions are made for the catechumens. These may replace the prayer of the faithful. If so, you should probably include a few of the universal intentions in this list, or replace some of these intentions with a few from the parish. In my parish, we usually prepare one set of intentions for all the weekend Masses. That way everyone prays for the catechumens, whether or not the rite of sending takes place at the Mass each one attends.

115. You conclude with a prayer. You stretch your hands out over the group while you recite the text.

116. You dismiss the elect if this takes place at Mass. Of course, you may keep them in church (C), but the ideal is that those to be baptized are excused at this time.

117. If this takes place at Sunday Mass, and if you are combining the intercessions, you start the creed right after the elect have left the room. Then the collection is taken up and the preparation of the altar and gifts begins. The reversal of these parts of the Mass is just enough to throw some ministers off balance. Let the ushers and musicians know about this sequence of events before Mass.

O K, here's another rite I don't like to do. It is optional, so you don't have to do it. It has been added to the *RCIA* in the United States. Many people love it and use it effectively, but I think it is inessential and gets in the way.

As the title indicates, this ceremony is for baptized candidates who are nearing their reception into the full communion of the Catholic Church. Ideally they should face "no greater burden than necessary" (473). They are already baptized. They have a foot in the door. When they are ready to be received, they should be admitted to the table of the Lord without delay. But the *RCIA* creates a series of optional rites to precede their reception. If overused they needlessly delay welcoming other Christians to share the Eucharist with us.

It is not clear why this group should go see the bishop. All of them are already baptized. They are not to be named among the elect, and the bishop's voice need not be invoked on behalf of this group. But the cathedral is a destination and any bishop carries celebrity status. Many people think of the cathedral ceremony as the time to "meet the bishop," which is a lovely thing to do, but it need not be a step that the baptized take on their road to the Eucharist.

As I will explain later, you may receive baptized Christians at any time of year. They don't have to wait until the Easter Vigil as catechumens should. Many of them should be received earlier. This rite, however, associates the treatment of candidates with the Easter timetable. It takes place prior to the cathedral liturgy, which almost always coincides with the First Sunday of Lent. So when you celebrate this rite of sending for your parish candidates, you imply that they will be received into the Church at Easter. They may, but there are reasons why that may not be a good idea. More on this later. I'm just trying to explain why I don't like doing this rite.

But in fairness, many baptized candidates have celebrated this rite to their spiritual benefit. It appears in the *RCIA*, so you certainly may use it.

The point of the ritual is similar to the rite of sending the catechumens to the rite of election: It alerts the parish community that future new members are rapidly approaching the sacraments of the Church. The newcomers will take part in an elaborate ceremony at the cathedral, and most of the parish will not be there. So this gives more members of the parish a chance to celebrate with the candidates.

438. This will probably take place at a parish Sunday Mass. If it doesn't, it's hard to understand why you would do this rite at all. Its purpose is to bridge the local parish community with the diocesan church represented by the bishop and the cathedral.

For this reason the scriptures will probably be those of that particular Sunday. The *RCIA* wants your homily to suit the occasion of this ritual. Quite honestly, I often deliver the same homily I give at other Masses that weekend. If I can make an allusion to the candidates, I will. But I believe the other parts of the ceremony adequately explain what is going on, and the homily I've prepared for the weekend will suit the situation just fine.

439. Someone presents the candidates to you. You invite them forward, and their names are called. This is similar to what happens in the rite of sending the catechumens. See the comments at 111.

Notice that the person giving the introduction has two options for explaining who the candidates are. One is that they are preparing for confirmation and Eucharist; the other is that they are preparing to be received into the full communion of the Catholic Church. The first group is baptized Catholics who never received religious formation or other sacraments. The second group is Christians who are not Catholics. The person giving the introduction may indicate who is who.

Sponsors guide the candidates forward, and they stand "before the celebrant." I would have them stand in the sanctuary facing the people. The ensuing dialogue still works.

440. You address everyone. You may use your own words. The sample text considers the two possibilities—you tell everyone whether the candidates are already Catholics who are preparing for confirmation and Communion, or if they are members of other Christian churches.

You ask the sponsors to give testimony. This rite does not mention godparents, but *RCIA* 404 does. That paragraph says that the candidates choose godparents for their formation. These may be newly selected for this purpose, or they may be the actual baptismal godparents, "provided they are truly capable of carrying out the responsibilities." Perhaps this phrase expresses the concern that the godparents did not support the catechesis expected after baptism. This paragraph was originally composed for Catholic candidates only. Its concern is that baptized Catholics have the assistance of godparents as they finally receive the catechesis they never had.

Other baptized Christians may or may not have godparents, and if they do, those godparents by definition belong to the Christian tradition in which the candidates were baptized, making them ineligible to serve as Catholic godparents. What these baptized candidates need more precisely is a Catholic sponsor for their reception into the full communion of the Catholic Church. That sponsor should have qualifications similar to those of a godparent for baptism in the Catholic Church (*CCL* 874/1).

So in *RCIA* 440, where you address the "sponsors," you may also be addressing the godparents of uncatechized Catholic candidates for confirmation and First Communion.

The suggested testimony for the sponsors is a simple affirmation to the question, "Do you consider them ready?" The questioning is much briefer than it is for the catechumens. The rite is drawing a distinction between the two groups by asking in broad terms if the sponsor considers the candidates ready. No detailed testimony is suggested. In the Catholic Church the baptized have a certain tendency though not an absolute right to the Eucharist, and the *RCIA* seems to respect this.

In practice, more testimony is and may be given. The entire rite is optional and you have some freedom to use similar words in many places. So, if you wanted to ask more questions of the sponsor, you could. Or if you wanted the sponsor to give a more detailed explanation of the person's spiritual progress, you could. Just be sure that sponsors know what is appropriate to say and what is not. It's best if they write it out ahead of time. You may receive the approval of the assembly as well. See the comments on 112 above (p. 51).

441. You accept the testimony and send the group to the bishop, who will exhort them to live as Christians. They do not leave yet—there are more prayers to follow, but you say the words of sending.

Note that baptized candidates do not sign the book of the elect (see 113). Signing the book is a prebaptismal ritual. It would be offensive to the baptismal status of the candidates to ask them to sign their names.

442. The general intercessions are offered. These are virtually identical to those for the rite of election (114). The only difference is that the second petition is expanded to pray not just for sponsors, but for godparents and sponsors. The similarity of the two sets of intercessions uncovers another problem with this ritual. Those who prepared these prayers did not recognize sufficient difference between the unbaptized and the baptized to create a new set of intentions for the latter. You are free to adapt these intercessions, eliminate several, and replace them with the prayer of the faithful from the other parish weekend Masses.

443. You stretch your hands out over the candidates and say a prayer for them. Once again, there is virtually no difference between this prayer and the one you say for the elect (115). I think this shows that the creators of this rite didn't put much thought into it. This prayer requests that God will "build (the candidates) into the kingdom of your Son," but as baptized members of the body of Christ, they already share in the kingdom of God.

444. If this didn't take place at a Sunday Mass, but at a word service, everyone is dismissed together, perhaps after singing a song. I think doing this as a word service misses the point. You want many people in the parish to see the candidates and to know they are nearing the end of their preparation. If you use this ceremony, it is more effective when it is done at Sunday Mass.

Notice that the rite does not suggest that the baptized candidates are dismissed while the Catholics remain for the Eucharist (see 116). The baptized have a place at the table, even if they are not sharing Communion from it.

445. The Liturgy of the Eucharist continues as usual. The rubrics say that you continue with the general intercessions of the Mass. You may, keeping the previous set of intercessions focused on the baptized candidates. But I think the double intercessions are a bit much, especially at Sunday Mass when many people are checking their watches. I would combine these groups of intercessions. Then lead the creed. (This reverses the order of these two parts of the Mass.) See the comments on 117 above, p. 53.

Parish Celebration for Sending Catechumens for Election and Candidates for Recognition by the Bishop
(RCIA 536–546)

By now you know what's coming: I really don't like this rite. First of all, I question the value of sending baptized candidates for recognition by the bishop. And I think the combined rites are difficult to negotiate in ways that respect the baptismal status of the candidates. This ceremony is optional. You do not have to do it for either group. But many parishes use it, and many catechumens and candidates have personally benefited from it.

It makes most sense to conduct this ceremony as part of a regularly scheduled Sunday Mass. That way more people in your parish can identify those who are nearing the completion of their formation, and be reminded to keep them in prayer. You may lead this ceremony at a word service, but it won't be as effective for the parish at large.

536. You will probably use the readings of the day and preach on them. The *RCIA* asks you to make special mention of the catechumens and the candidates. If you can do so briefly and connect it to your homily, do it. I often preach my regular homily for the weekend and trust the ceremony to explain the rest; see 438.

537–539. The groups are handled separately. The catechumens are introduced, and their godparents are asked for testimony. If the signing of names takes place in the parish, that happens next. This section borrows word-for-word from 111–113. See p. 50 above for comments.

540–542. The candidates are introduced, their sponsors are asked for testimony, and you conclude with some remarks. This directly quotes 439–441. See p. 55 above for comments.

543–544. The intercessions are virtually the same as in 114–115 and 442–443. No real distinction is made between catechumens and candidates.

545. The catechumens may be dismissed, but the candidates are not. In practice, many candidates prefer to be dismissed together with the catechumens. They would like the extra time to reflect on the word of God and the ceremony they have just experienced. It also makes the "sending" more of a sending. So if my candidates ask to be dismissed, I let them leave. But as baptized members of the body of Christ, they are entitled to a place among the faithful at Sunday Mass.

If this is a word service, everyone is dismissed, and a song may be sung. But that defeats the purpose of this ceremony, which will have more effect if it is celebrated at a parish Sunday Mass.

546. Conclude with the Liturgy of the Eucharist. For comments about the general intercessions and the creed, see 117 and 445.

Calling the Candidates to Continuing Conversion (RCIA 450–458)

This is another optional ceremony. It was conceived for use in the United States in situations when you have no catechumens, but you do have baptized candidates preparing to receive confirmation and Eucharist. The rite allows you to call them to continuing conversion without having them recognized by the bishop. If you use this rite, there is no point in celebrating the rite of *sending* for this group (p. 54). You are not sending them anywhere. They will celebrate the call to continuing conversion right there at their parish home.

The existence of this rite illustrates that baptized Christians need not present themselves to the local bishop for admission to the Catholic Eucharistic table. They may fulfill all that is required of them through the parish church.

The rite is designed for baptized but previously uncatechized adults who are entering their final Lent before being received into the Church or completing their initiation as Catholics. Although the rite says that Easter is a laudable occasion for the confirmation and Communion of previously baptized Catholics (409), the reception of other Christians into the full communion of the Catholic Church may take place at any time of year. Consequently, there may be little use for this as a parish rite near the beginning of Lent.

Besides, if candidates for reception into the Catholic Church are ready, they need no other preliminary rites. This ceremony is optional; if such candidates have advanced this far, they may well be ready for their reception. No other ceremony and no other Lent needs to separate them from Communion.

That being said, many baptized candidates find the calling to continuing conversion an impressive ceremony when they celebrate it at the cathedral, and there's no reason why some would not also find it impressive in the parish. If for various reasons you think it is advisable for the candidates and the people to celebrate this rite in your parish, you may do so. But it's optional.

The celebrant is the pastor (448). The parochial vicar and the deacon are not to preside for this rite. This probably reaffirms the pastor's role as leader of the congregation and representative of the bishop.

450. The readings will probably be those of the day. You will probably celebrate this on a Sunday just before the beginning of Lent, or perhaps on the First Sunday of Lent if there are no catechumens. Your homily may explain what is happening and why, and it should touch the hearts of all the faithful, not just the candidates.

451. The person in charge of the candidates' formation introduces the rite. You could introduce this person yourself, or he or she could begin by giving his or her name and position. That way the people in the congregation know who is speaking to them and why.

A sample text is given. The person addresses you as "Reverend Father." I don't know about you, but no one addresses me as "Reverend Father." You may be addressed in the way you are normally addressed by your people.

The words "since Easter is drawing near" are in parentheses, implying that the rite could be conducted at some other time of year. But 448 clearly states that it is celebrated at the beginning of Lent, and the remainder of the rite refers several times to the Lent/Easter cycle.

The other parenthetical options in the sample text make adjustments for the nature of these candidates. If they are baptized, previously uncatechized Catholics, they seek to complete their Christian initiation and are to be admitted to confirmation and the Eucharist. If they are Christians of other denominations, they are preparing to be received into the full communion of the Church and full Eucharistic sharing.

You invite them forward, together with their sponsors. For the sake of participation I usually have them stand facing the people, not necessarily facing me.

Someone calls their names. Probably this will be the person who just made the introduction. Whoever does it should know how to pronounce the list correctly.

452. You have the sponsors and perhaps the assembly affirm the progress of the candidates. Some deliberation should have taken place beforehand. This paragraph refers you to *RCIA* 122, but that describes the situation of unbaptized catechumens. If these candidates have made similar catechetical progress, they are probably ready for full communion, not merely for this preliminary rite.

If you have been part of the deliberation yourself, you use a version of 452A. You are giving your own testimony about the spiritual progress your candidates have made. You ask the sponsors to verify this, and they do.

453. If you were not part of the deliberations, use a version of 453B, which assigns you more questions for the sponsors. In this case, you rely on others to give the testimony that you cannot authentically give.

Either version of this allows you to elicit approval from the entire community as well. You may ask everyone if they assent to the testimony of the sponsors. This is optional because in reality only a handful of people in the community may be able to give this testimony authentically. I would probably ask those who know the candidates personally to stand and testify. You could do this for each candidate individually or for all of them as a group. See comments at 112 (p. 51).

454. You make the act of recognition. You recognize the desire of the candidates, you invite them into Lent with a spirit of repentance, and you ask them to be faithful to their baptismal covenant.

This is supposed to be the highlight of the ceremony. To me, it isn't much of a highlight, and it shows the weakness of this optional rite. You are telling the candidates the same thing you tell everyone else: Engage in this Lent as responsible Christians. The only difference is that you say, "the Church recognizes your desire." Sorry, but this should have been obvious a long time ago, and it isn't enough to support an entire ritual. You may do this ritual if you like, but I think its meaning is rather thin.

I digress. The candidates respond, "Thanks be to God," and you give instructions to the sponsors, who make some gesture of care. An embrace usually works just fine. A hand on the shoulder also suffices. Even a handshake will do the trick. It should be a sincere indication of the relationship between each pair of people.

455. These general intercessions are the prayer of the faithful for the Mass. In other similar rites you have the option of praying two sets of intentions, but this rite envisions one set that will include the prayers for the Church and the whole world. You may select one or more of the intentions from this list and add them to the others for the weekend. It wouldn't hurt to pray for these candidates at every parish Mass this weekend.

456. When you give the final prayer, stretch your hands out over the group of candidates. This prayer doubles as the prayer that concludes the prayer of the faithful.

457. If this takes place at a word service and not at Sunday Mass, you dismiss everyone at the same time. You may all sing a final song.

458. But more likely this will take place at Sunday Mass or some other Mass, and you move along with the preparation of the gifts.

The rubrics never tell you what to do about the creed. You could insert it before the intercessions. That would be the most logical place. Or you could recite it after the intercessions, which is the pattern in the rites of sending. Or you could omit it, which is permitted in other rites like this. It's your choice.

Scrutiny
(RCIA 150–156,
164–177)

The scrutinies are a special series of Lenten prayers for those to be baptized at Easter. They uncover and heal what is weak and sinful, and they strengthen what is strong and good (141). There are three of them, and they should not be omitted without serious reason. Reducing the number of scrutinies is a dispensation the *bishop* may grant, not the local priest (20).

The scrutinies include an exorcism. When most people hear this word, they think of a Hollywood-style demonic possession. This exorcism is not so dramatic, and it does not presume that Satan has taken over the entire will of the persons in question. The exorcism does presume, though, that Satan has some power.

Underlying the exorcism is the assumption that baptism makes a difference in someone's moral culpability. After you are baptized, you are a member of the body of Christ. You have the gift of God's grace every day of your life. The Holy Spirit will help you make good decisions, based on the Christian life you share. If you sin, it's your own fault. You did not take advantage of the spiritual help that has been with you all along.

Life is different for the unbaptized. They have not enjoyed the benefits of sanctifying grace as you have. Consequently, their sin is not entirely their fault. They are more subject to the temptations of this world. The baptized who sin seek forgiveness. The unbaptized who sin get an exorcism. Wrongdoing for the unbaptized has a devil-made-me-do-it quality.

Still, many people complain about the titles of these prayers. "Come to Mass for a scrutiny and exorcism" is hardly a cozy invitation. But these titles are quite ancient in the Christian liturgy, even though they have not been widely used in recent years in the West. Both words have scriptural roots. Exorcism was part of Jesus' ministry, and Psalm 139 sings of how God scrutinizes the believer—God understands us through and through.

Prior to the Council, the exorcisms were addressed to the devil. The priest commanded the devil to leave the person preparing for baptism. In the restoration of the catechumenate, such deprecations were evaluated and found wanting. It seemed more in keeping with modern sensibilities and more descriptive of the power of Christ to make Jesus the recipient of these words. We no longer bother addressing Satan directly; we address Christ directly because his power is stronger than evil.

The scrutiny Masses could be the first time you publicly pray over those to be baptized. The rite of acceptance is often celebrated at Sunday Mass, but it was designed as a word service. The rite of sending is optional. The rite of election usually takes place at the cathedral. You may have dismissed catechumens from the weekly liturgy with an exorcism or blessing. But the scrutinies are the first major rites that are expected to take place during a parish Mass on Sunday.

Normally you celebrate these scrutinies on the Third, Fourth, and Fifth Sundays of Lent. If for some extraordinary reason you are baptizing adults on an occasion apart from Easter, you celebrate the scrutinies prior to that. For good reason you may celebrate the scrutinies on a weekday, but this is not ideal. The Lectionary foresees the possibility, nonetheless, and gives you "optional Masses" for weeks three, four and five of Lent (236, 243, and 250). These texts may replace those of another weekday during those weeks, but they were inserted into the Lectionary for the sake of celebrating the scrutinies. These prayers are so important that the Lectionary bends over backward to give you ample opportunity to celebrate them on behalf of your elect.

Some people ask why there are three scrutinies instead of one. One theory holds that that's the wrong question. The real question should be, "Why are there three scrutinies instead of six?" In some ancient traditions there were quite a number of scrutinies and exorcisms in the weeks prior to baptism. But as the calendar evolved with the rite of election on the First

Sunday of Lent, Ember Days on the Second Sunday, and Palm Sunday on the sixth, there was room for only three scrutinies in Lent.

The presidential prayers for these Masses are not those of the Lent Sunday, but the scrutiny prayers from the Ritual Masses in the back of the *Roman Missal*. Look up For the Conferral of the Sacraments of Christian Initiation: For the Celebration of the Scrutinies, and you will find the texts for the collect, the prayer over the offerings, and the prayer after communion. The recommended antiphons for the entrance and communion of this Mass are also found there; they might inspire your musicians to choose appropriate selections. You will also find an insertion for the Eucharistic prayer on the same page.

150, 164, 171. The readings are supposed to be those in the Lectionary under Ritual Masses: Catechumenate and Christian Initiation of Adults (745, 746, and 747). Those numbers refer you to numbers 28, 31, and 34, which are the Year A readings for the Third, Fourth, and Fifth Sundays of Lent. The revised *Roman Missal* acknowledges that you may celebrate the scrutinies on weekdays, but the Gospels should always be those of the aforementioned Sundays. Apparently the other readings are more negotiable.

Many priests object to this. It means that in Years B and C of the cycle, you use one set of readings at the scrutiny Masses, and another set at the other Masses. It means different music, a different responsorial psalm, and a different homily. Readers, cantors, and deacons need to be told which readings to use for which Mass. It can be a mess.

But it is what the Church desires. The texts of the scrutinies rely heavily upon these Gospels for the integration of the liturgy. After you proclaim the Gospel, you lead the scrutiny.

151, 165, 172. You preach a homily about the meaning of the scrutiny in light of the spiritual journey of the elect. This presents a practical problem in Years B and C—how to preach effectively with a different set of readings at some weekend Masses? There are several solutions:

• If you have more than one priest or deacon in the parish, have someone prepare the homily for the scrutiny and someone else preach the other Masses.

• Prepare a homily that works for all the Masses by adjusting part of the text.

• Preach about some other part of the liturgy, not the readings—such as the penitential act, the creed, or part of the Eucharistic prayer.

• Or, taking a lead from the *Roman Missal*, preach on one of the first two readings or the psalm, not on the Gospel. Switch the *Gospel* for the scrutiny Masses, but keep the other readings. The scrutiny prayers will make more sense, and you won't have to revise your homily very much.

• Bite the bullet and prepare two separate homilies.

You need a way to give the liturgy its due while also taking care of yourself. Your people and your catechumens will be grateful for the time and attention you give your preaching for these special events.

152, 166, 173. The elect and their godparents come forward and stand before you. The rubrics do not say how they get there. Are you supposed to invite them up? Does someone on the catechumenate team do this? Are the godparents told in advance what to do so that no invitation needs to be made? Personally, I like the last of these possibilities. The fewer words the better.

Usually I want the elect to be facing the people, but if they are going to kneel for the next prayer, it might be better if they face the sanctuary for this ritual. Godparents will need to place a hand on the shoulder of the elect, so they should take a position nearby. If the godparent escorts the elect into position now by placing a hand on the shoulder already, it will help establish respective roles.

In some churches the elect and godparents move in pairs into the aisles instead of the sanctuary. This makes sense only if it improves visibility. If arranging the elect this way helps the assembly see what is going on, you could try this. But really, there isn't that much to see, and having the elect stand "before the celebrant" as the rite suggests will usually create a suitable image.

You ask everyone to pray in silence that the elect will have a spirit of repentance, a sense of sin, and the freedom of the children of God. Then you ask the elect to pray in silence and to bow or kneel. You use your own words.

All pray in silence. The rubrics can be read to mean that the faithful pray in silence first, and then the elect pray in silence second. But I think this flows better if you address both groups in a two-part instruction, and then have everyone observe silence together.

In some parishes, everyone kneels for this silent prayer. I guess you could, but the prayer is going to be focused on the elect. The faithful are praying for them, so a difference in posture between the two groups helps demonstrate the separate roles.

The problem is that the faithful may still be seated. There is no instruction for them to change posture after the homily. In fact, this paragraph says that the period of silence concludes when the elect *and* the faithful stand. Practically speaking, many congregations will stand when this ceremony begins because that's what they are accustomed to do after the homily. You have a choice here. You could invite people to pray in silence while seated, or you could have them stand to pray. In either case, the end of silence is signaled by having everyone stand together.

153, 167, 174. Intercessions are made for the elect. You introduce these, and another minister leads the petitions. It happens the same way the prayer of the faithful does on a typical Sunday. You have the option of blending the parish's prayer of the faithful with these petitions. They serve separate purposes: These are expressly for the elect, and the others are for the Church and the world. I usually combine the petitions, but you are free to do them separately.

The *RCIA* gives you two sets of sample intercessions. The second set uses images from the Gospel and is especially effective in tying themes together. You may adapt the intercessions to fit your circumstances.

The godparent stands with his or her right hand on the shoulder of the elect. Someone should probably give them this instruction before the service begins so you do not have to give directions during the ceremony. The fewer words you say, the more impact the ritual words will have.

The North American Forum on the Catechumenate has promoted a preparatory process that elicits heartfelt spiritual needs from the elect and inserts them as the petitions of a gripping litany. To be sure, these intentions will have more integrity if they reflect the personal journey of the elect. A catechist can help with this by asking at a catechetical session prior to each scrutiny such leading questions as "How are you thirsting for living water?" "To what are you blind?" "To what must you die in order to rise again?" The same questions may be asked of our society in general. As the elect wrestle with these questions, their deepest spiritual hungers can be made manifest.

A good writer can transform these hungers into intercessions for the elect—maintaining an appropriate level of decorum and anonymity on their behalf. In this way, the elect hear the community praying for them week by week for the specific needs they have voiced.

There are various musical settings for such petitions. These can be very effective. Some litanies are so insistent that they carry the emotional power of driving evil away by fervent, confident prayer. You have some freedom with these petitions, and they can become an effective tool to set the stage for the exorcism. But you may also execute these intercessions in the same way you do them every week. Nothing special needs to happen. After all, the faithful should be vigorous in their prayer whether or not the elect are present.

154, 168, 175. The exorcism is in three parts. You address a prayer to God, you impose hands if possible, and then you address a prayer to Christ. Because the imposition of hands traditionally invokes the Holy Spirit, the exorcism has a trinitarian content.

You have two options for these prayers. Both of them rely on the Lent Gospels of Year A in the Lectionary cycle.

In the first part, you keep your hands joined while saying the prayer to God. Your hands will be in three different positions throughout this exorcism. The rubric says you face the elect—probably because the prayer is about them, and it should be clear whom you are praying for. This first prayer is introductory. It does pray for deliverance, but not as strongly as the final element of the exorcism does.

After this first prayer, you impose hands on each of the elect if this can be done conveniently. The number or placement of the elect could make this difficult, but for the sake of the symbol, it is worth the effort for you to walk around the group and place your hands on the heads of each. Some parishes keep the elect kneeling throughout this time of prayer. You could argue that kneeling is a posture for penitence and fits the spirit of these prayers, and that the adaptations encouraged for the intercessions could also apply to posture. But the rubrics call for kneeling earlier on, and standing during the imposition of hands.

Some priests have invited other helpers to impose hands as well, notably the catechist and the godparent. This is not foreign to the spirit of the exorcism. After all, everyone should be praying silently together with you, and the particular roles of the catechist and godparent need to be expressed in some way before the entire community. Catechists are supposed to have an active role in the rites (16). The godparent has already been cued to place a hand on the shoulder of the elect, so it is not out of place to have them place hands on the head. In any event, everyone should be praying fervently and sincerely for the conversion of the elect.

Finally you stretch your hands out over the entire group while you pronounce the prayer to Christ. This is the meat of the exorcism. All the versions of this prayer appeal for the overthrow of the spirit of evil and the entrance of the Holy Spirit. They sum up why this period of final preparation for baptism is called "purification and enlightenment." They purify the elect from what is evil, and they enlighten them with what is good.

A song may be sung to complete the scrutiny, and a number of psalms are recommended, including 139, which gives the scrutiny its name. It could be effective to have a short piece of music conclude the ceremony, letting everyone give voice to its meaning. But you know how things are on Sunday mornings—most folks are anxious to move on with the Mass as they know and love it, so that they can return to the other demands of their day. If something needs to be cut from the scrutiny, this song is expendable.

155, 169, 176. You dismiss the elect. If this takes place at a word service, everyone is dismissed together. For serious reasons you may invite the elect to stay, but it is best to dismiss them while Mass continues.

The first option addresses those who have just been prayed over as the "elect" and—for the first two scrutinies—it invites them back for another one. The second option directly borrows the dismissal from 67, including the rubric that calls the group "catechumens." It means the elect. Of course, if you have catechumens who will not become elect until next Lent, they are also dismissed at this time. Option C is for those circumstances when the elect are not dismissed, and option D is used at a word service, after which everyone leaves together.

156, 170, 177. If Mass continues, and if the prayer of the faithful was not incorporated into the intercessions for the elect, it comes next. It is not clear why this prayer should come before the creed. This may be an oversight in the text.

You may omit the general intercessions and the creed for pastoral reasons. Personally, I like to combine the intercessions for the elect with the prayer of the faithful, and recite the creed right after the dismissal. A lot of priests omit the creed on occasions like this, but it only takes a minute or two, it gives everyone a chance to participate together (even those who refuse to sing), it anchors us in our faith, it expresses our unity with other believers, and it distinguishes us from the elect who were just dismissed.

The *Roman Missal* recommends that the Apostles' Creed be used during the seasons of Lent and Easter (Order of Mass 19). It is called the "baptismal creed" of the early church because it evolved from the baptismal promises. By reciting the Apostles' Creed during Lent, the faithful are preparing to witness the baptisms at the Easter Vigil and to renew their own baptismal promises the same night.

During the Eucharistic Prayer, you pray for the godparents by name. The *Roman Missal* offers a complete formula for Eucharistic Prayer I, but given the length of that prayer and of the entire Mass, few priests probably use it. The Missal's formulas for prayers II and III do not prompt you to mention the godparents by name, but it would keep the spirit of the prayer if you did. People rarely get mentioned by name in the Eucharistic Prayer, so this is an unusual honor bestowed upon those who are guiding new Christians to the font, table, and life of the community.

Penitential Rites (Scrutinies) for Children (RCIA 295–303)

If you have children of catechetical age preparing for baptism, they may celebrate scrutinies adapted to their understanding. The *RCIA* calls them "penitential rites"—perhaps because the word "scrutiny" may sound too frightening to children. These rites are modeled after those for adults; see p. 65.

The *RCIA* envisions that these children may be of an age at which their peers are preparing for First Communion. Consequently, these penitential rites offer an occasion for baptized children to celebrate reconciliation for the first time (293, 302–303). Before the liturgy ends, the unbaptized children may be dismissed, while the rest remain behind for confession. There is no precedent for this in the history of the catechumenate, and it is a little odd. Obviously, the modern framers of the rite were trying to adapt for children the experience of adult catechumens being dismissed after the scrutiny as the faithful continue with the Eucharist. If the baptized children in the group had still not made their First Communion, they would only be eligible for reconciliation. I'm sure this idea looked good to the committee when they got it on paper, but it has no precise ritual precedent. I doubt that it gets used very much.

Although adults celebrate three scrutinies, only one or perhaps two penitential rites are envisioned for children (294). The framers of the revised catechumenate feared that three scrutinies would be too much for children, but in many parishes children are invited to all three scrutinies for adults and seem to do fine with them. Indeed, the scrutinies intensify their understanding that their upcoming baptism is quite important.

In my parish, whenever we have children catechumens, I usually don't use this rite. We invite children to the scrutinies with the adults at a parish Sunday Mass, but you could have a separate ceremony just for kids apart from Mass—even on a weekday in Lent, at an assembly of students in a Catholic school, for example.

295. You gather all the unbaptized and baptized children of the catechetical group together and explain the ceremony to them: All will experience God's mercy, but in different ways. I would probably start with a greeting such as, "The Lord be with you," but the rubrics do not explicitly call for that.

After this introduction a song may be sung. Most communities would probably start with the song, but the intent here is to make sure the children know what is happening before they start doing any of it.

296. You offer a prayer. Two options are given. Choose one. They make similar petitions. One is shorter than the other.

297. You have quite a selection of readings to draw from, including the three Gospels from the adult scrutinies. If more than one reading is used, a psalm may also be sung. Depending on the age of the children, one reading may suffice. The *Directory for Masses with Children* permits dividing one reading among several readers, as is done for the Passion in Holy Week (*DMC* 47; see also *Lectionary for Masses with Children* 52).

298. You explain the readings in your homily. Keep it focused on the children, and speak to them in a way they can understand.

You lead an examination of conscience right after the homily—or you may incorporate it into your words.

If the baptized are going to receive the sacrament of penance for the first time, you invite them to show a sign of their faith and sorrow. It is not clear what sign this might be. It could simply be kneeling for a while. But if you have another creative idea that makes sense to children, use it.

299. You introduce the intercessions. These have been adapted for children, and you may adapt them again. You may use the ones from the adult scrutinies for inspiration.

Personally, I think these sample petitions speak what adults wish children would feel rather than what children actually feel. They read as though they are trying to induce guilt where none may be felt. If you like them, use them, but if you can do better, write your own.

300. The threefold form of the exorcism of adults is abandoned here in favor of a simpler structure. Two options are given, and you stretch out your hands over the group while you say either one.

The first is adopted from the rite of baptism for children. It is one version of the prayer of exorcism that follows the intercessions. The only difference is that this one does not refer to original sin. Infants have committed no personal sin, so their exorcism is about original sin. However, children of catechetical age are more responsible for their actions, so original sin is not so much an issue here as personal sin.

In the other option, you divide your prayer with the children, who testify to their spiritual progress while you ask God to free them from evil that could harm them. This prayer is not as explicit as the exorcisms in the adult rite. It aims to be more understandable to children.

301. You anoint the children with the oil of catechumens or you impose hands on them. The rubrics say you omit the anointing if they have already received it, but elsewhere you are permitted to anoint catechumens more than once (100). The structure imitates the rite of baptism for children, in which an anointing follows the prayer of exorcism. In the adult scrutinies, no anointing is included.

Some people find the anointing another oddity about this ritual, but I actually like it. There is strong evidence in the history of the catechumenate that anointings accompanied exorcisms. Once you expelled the evil spirit and summoned the Holy Spirit, you sealed the good Spirit in with oil. The anointing makes this spirit transfusion stick. Perhaps in some future revision of the adult rites, an anointing could return to the scrutinies.

If you are low on the oil of catechumens, you may bless more yourself. A text is provided. You do not have to use oil blessed by the bishop when you are anointing catechumens before baptism. Canon 847/1 says you may use any vegetable oil, but olive oil is traditional.

As you anoint the children, you use the text from the rite of baptism for children. You anoint the breast (the collarbone area), hands, or other parts of the body. When dealing with children, hands are probably safest, but talk it over with parents and catechists before making your choice.

A blessing of the catechumens may follow the anointing (97), to balance the exorcism that preceded it.

Alternatively, you may lay hands on the children. The same option exists in the rite of baptism for children, where the anointing may be omitted if the number of children is large, if it would delay the liturgy unduly, or if there is some other good reason; see p. 147. If you choose this option, speak the text, and impose hands on the head of each child.

As you can see, the exorcism and anointing of children (300–301) is inspired more by the exorcism of infants (*RBC* 49–51) than by the exorcism of adults (for example, *RCIA* 153–154).

302. You may dismiss the children. If they leave now, you use option A. If you are keeping them in place until after hearing the confessions of their friends, use option B.

303. You hear the confessions of the baptized children. You give an introduction, hear the children first and then everyone else. It is not clear why you should hear confessions in two groups. Normally people may confess in any order. A song concludes the celebration.

This entire liturgy seems like a hodgepodge, but it might just work effectively with careful planning. You could also think of it as a penance service for children at which some special prayers will be said for those who are unbaptized. It could make a suitable prayer service during the season of Lent if it is carefully crafted for children.

But for scrutinies, I usually invite children to participate on Sunday with the adults.

If you have baptized candidates preparing for reception into the Church, confirmation, Communion, or some combination of these at the Easter Vigil, you may lead them through a penitential rite on the Second Sunday of Lent. You may also choose a Lenten weekday. If the candidates are to receive sacraments on an occasion apart from the Easter Vigil, you may celebrate this penitential rite at any time. It was created for use in the United States; it is not offered in many other parts of the world, and it is optional even in the United States.

The structure of the penitential rite parallels that of the scrutiny; see p. 65. It was probably designed for the Second Sunday of Lent because it was the only date not taken by the rite of election, the scrutinies, and Palm Sunday. There is no historical precedent for this penitential rite, no tradition behind linking the Gospel of the Transfiguration with those preparing to be received into the full communion of the Catholic Church. It is a new creation.

I occasionally use this rite, but I prefer to opt out of it. I think it contributes to the false equalization of candidates and catechumens. Still, it has been celebrated profitably by candidates, who speak well of the experience.

The *RCIA* does not offer a combined scrutiny for catechumens and candidates. This is the only significant place where the book insists on keeping the groups separate. A scrutiny is a prebaptismal liturgy, and it should not be offered to those already baptized. The penitential rite offers a parallel rite to candidates, separating them by a week from the scrutinies of the elect. However, the structure is so similar that the distinctions between the two rites are otherwise difficult to grasp.

The rite is "penitential" and not a scrutiny because the texts presume that the baptized are guiltier of their offenses than the unbaptized are. The baptized should know better, and they have the grace of their baptism to help them through times of temptation. But the unbaptized do not have those spiritual helps, so they undergo an exorcism to lighten the power of the world's false lures.

The rite is tricky to negotiate. On one hand, you want to encourage the baptized to acknowledge their sins before receiving the sacraments of the Church. They should do this formally by celebrating the sacrament of reconciliation prior to Easter. This penitential rite may help them prepare their hearts to confess their sins to a priest.

On the other hand, in the case of candidates baptized in other Churches, you don't want it to appear as though they need to repent of the "sin" of belonging to another denomination before joining the Catholic Church. Catholics used to think that way, but our thought has evolved through the ecumenical movement and the postconciliar revision of our rites.

The introduction to the penitential rite says it takes place in a word service (459), but the rite offers the option of celebrating it during Mass (472).

464. You welcome the people. I would probably begin with a greeting such as, "The Lord be with you."

You introduce the rite by explaining its meaning. It is a celebration of the comforting message of pardon for sin. You may use your own words; no sample text is offered.

A song may be sung. This feels backwards. Shouldn't the song precede the greeting and introduction? Yes, and if this takes place during Sunday Mass that would happen unquestionably. All would sing a hymn, and then you would make the sign of the cross, greet the people, and give the introduction noted above. The transposition of the song is apparently borrowed from the description of the penitential rite (scrutiny) for children of catechetical age (295; see p. 74). In that case, however, you explain things informally to the children before they enter worship. A different strategy would seem more fitting for adults.

465. You say the prayer for the Second Sunday of Lent, but if this rite is celebrated on another day or in a word service apart from Mass, you may use the prayer printed here. No mention is made of the penitental act from the opening rites of the Mass. The creators of this rite may have thought that the penitental act should be omitted to avoid the redundancy of celebrating a penitential rite after the homily. Or this could be an oversight. If you celebrate this at a Sunday Mass, you would logically include the penitential act as always.

466. The readings come from the Second Sunday of Lent if you are celebrating this rite on that day. Otherwise, you may choose texts from another part of the Lectionary. See for example the readings for Masses for the remission of sins (*LM* 946–952).

467. You preach about the readings, the need for repentance, and the significance of the ceremony about to unfold.

468. The candidates and their sponsors come forward. The rubrics do not say how they get there. I like it when the sponsors bring them forward without any introduction or further cue. But you may invite them forward in your own words, or have a catechist do so.

As in the scrutinies (152, 166, 173), you invite the congregation to pray silently that the candidates will repent and receive the freedom of the children of God. You invite the candidates to bow or kneel and pray silently as well. It works better if you give both these instructions together, and then pause for silent prayer, rather than pausing for silence twice: first for the congregation to pray and then again for the candidates to pray.

After this, everyone stands for the intercessions. Presumably, the congregation has remained seated after the homily, and they now stand. Sometimes they spontaneously stand when you begin this rite. It's all right for them to stand for their silent prayer while the candidates kneel. But when the silence is over, all stand.

In some parishes, the candidates are invited to remain kneeling through the intercessions as a sign of their repentance. You have some freedom because this rite allows adaptation, but I think it's better for them to stand.

469. The intercessions may be combined with the prayer of the faithful if this rite is celebrated at Mass; see 153, 167, 174. In that case, add the parish's intentions to those for the candidates. You may always compose your own intentions for the Mass, so even though the rubrics do not tell you that in this paragraph, you still have the option of choosing some of the intentions from this list, changing the wording, or writing your own petitions.

Your introduction to these intercessions suggests you call the candidates by name. It is a good idea to announce their names as often as possible. If nothing else, it will make you learn who they are. The words "sealed with the gift of the Father" are in parentheses for the rare circumstance when one or more of the candidates has a valid confirmation but is now preparing for Communion. Those joining the Catholic Church from an Eastern Orthodox Church would have received a valid confirmation at their baptism, but they would have received a valid Eucharist as well. Adults baptized Roman Catholic and who are already confirmed, but have never received First Communion, would not be receiving confirmation a second time. But those cases are rare.

Some of the petitions are drawn from the rite of election and the call to continuing conversion; others were composed for this rite. An assisting minister reads them—the deacon or reader or whoever reads petitions at your parish.

If you are writing your own petitions, you may obtain ideas from the candidates themselves. In a catechetical session prior to the penitential rite, you or a catechist can visit with them about what they are trying to leave behind this Lent. If what they share can be transformed into generic petitions, the candidates will recognize that the community is praying for their own struggles as they undergo the rigors of Lent.

470. You lead a prayer that strongly resembles the exorcism of the unbaptized (154, 168, 175). You start with a prayer to God, impose hands on the candidates, and then with hands outstretched over them you pray to Jesus. This is the three-part trinitarian formula so evident in the scrutinies. The texts are different. Version A especially refers to the gospel of the Second Sunday of Lent. In both cases the second prayer, the one addressed to Jesus, does not include an exorcism. It does not pray for the removal of any evil spirit. Instead, it prays for "the power of [God's] Spirit," for healing, guidance, and safety. These affable prayers resemble the style but not the bold purpose of exorcisms.

You may conclude these prayers with a song. The same psalms recommended for scrutinies appear here. But no song may be necessary. It is optional.

471. If this takes place at a word service you dismiss the entire group and everyone may sing a song; see 155, 169, 176.

472. If it takes place at Mass, continue as usual; see 156, 170, 177. The profession of faith could be omitted, but I think it's a good idea to include it. The baptized have already professed their faith in the statements of the creed, so professing it together with everyone will affirm their baptism.

You don't have to combine the intercessions for the elect with the prayer of the faithful. If you do the prayer of the faithful separately, it would follow the creed.

Once you get to the collection and the procession of the gifts, you're home free. There are no other changes to this Mass.

Presentations
(RCIA 157–163,
178–184)

During the season of Lent the Church offers two presentations to the elect: one of the creed and the other of the Lord's Prayer. Ordinarily, these should not be omitted, though they rank less important than the scrutinies.

These rites are quite ancient. There are references to them clear back to the third, fourth, and fifth centuries. Through them the Church offered its treasures to those who were preparing for baptism. To this day, we regard them as prebaptismal rituals.

Early Christians presented the creed to those who were completing their preparation for baptism. The unbaptized were not allowed to know the creed. The creed was also called the "symbol" and retained some mystique. It was not to be shared with non-Christians because they lacked the expertise and the faith to understand it. Sharing the creed with the wrong crowd subjected it to ridicule. This is why the creed still belongs to the second half of the Mass. In the early church, those who were not yet believers were dismissed after the Liturgy of the Word. The first thing the faithful did upon the departure of the catechumens was to recite the creed that bonded them and that established their credentials for sharing the Eucharist.

The early Christians never wrote down the creed. They feared it might fall into the wrong hands and be used to extend persecution.

Those who had undergone catechesis received the creed as a summary of their beliefs and a preparation for their baptism. The creed was handed on after the first scrutiny. Catechumens did not receive it until they had been spiritually scrubbed in preparation.

The presentation of the creed started a trajectory that the early church completed at the other end of Lent. The elect received the creed early in the season; they reflected on it and memorized it during the weeks of Lent; they recited it from memory at the end of Lent; and as they approached the waters of baptism, they were asked to profess their faith in the creed point by point. After they accomplished all that, they were baptized.

Even today, handing over the creed is a significant step in the formation of catechumens. It sets the tone for the kind of preparation that Lent entails. It purifies and enlightens. It is a turning away from former allegiances and turning toward Christ. The creed is key to the enlightenment phase of this period. Some of the first catechists engaged the elements of the creed as a springboard for prebaptismal catechetical sessions.

The presentation of the Lord's Prayer also dates to the early church, although the Lord's Prayer was not considered as secret as the creed was. After all, the Lord's Prayer comes from the Gospels, and catechumens had been hearing the Gospels for some time. There is no historical evidence for catechumens reciting the Lord's Prayer back to the community, as they had to recite the creed. The giving back of the Lord's Prayer took place during the baptismal Eucharist, when the newly baptized recited it together with the faithful to prepare for Communion. "Give us today our daily bread" had Eucharistic resonances, and it still does.

The presentations may be offered during the period of the catechumenate (79, 104–105, 147) instead of during Lent. This is new to the history of the catechumenate. All the past evidence for these presentations makes them part of the immediate preparation for baptism. However, when the catechumenate was revised after the Council, parishes received the option of celebrating the presentations earlier—long before the scrutinies. The reason was that the framers of the modern catechumenate thought Lent was getting overburdened with rituals. Election, the scrutinies, and the preparation rites all needed space, and some thought that the insertion of the two presentations would be too much. So you now have the option of celebrating them earlier.

The *Ceremonial of Bishops* (*CB*) takes a dim view of this, however. It encourages the bishop to celebrate the presentations, but only if they follow the rite of election (421).

I'm of two minds about this. I hate to break a long historical tradition. If celebrating the presentations in the midst of everything else during Lent was good enough for our ancestors, it's good enough for me. However, it is a bit artificial. The creed is no big secret any more. Anyone can find it in the nearest participation aid or Web site. You'd think catechumens would want to have it in hand a lot sooner in their preparation, so they could see in summary what it was they were going to be asked about before baptism. It would also help them center themselves when they get caught by the flurry of media-friendly Catholic controversies: celibacy, devotion to Mary, birth control, abortion, remarriage, and sacramental reconciliation, to name a few. All these are important matters, but they are not part of the creed. Even the real presence of Christ in the Eucharist—central as it is to Catholic faith—is not in the creed. But the Resurrection is. So is the Incarnation. So is life everlasting. By reinforcing what is at the heart of Catholic belief, it becomes a lot easier to weather the storms surrounding controversial matters. Besides, some unbaptized people already hold the basic tenets of the creed, and have done so long before they appear at our catechetical sessions. So handing on the creed would seem to be a logical thing earlier in their formation. Still, I kind of like it at the end—it brings things to a grand head, and it sets a theme for the season of Lent, a season of deepening belief.

Most everyone knows the Lord's Prayer, of course, so here again it is a bit artificial to present it to the elect as though they'd never heard it before in their lives. It is a prayer that they have probably used quite a bit already, especially in catechetical sessions. So, you could present it earlier. I still like it late in the process, as a prelude to the Eucharist. The presentation of the creed functions as a prebaptismal rite, and the presentation of the Lord's Prayer as a pre-Eucharistic rite.

In fact, I usually blend this second presentation with the preparation rites on Holy Saturday morning. I'll explain more of that later, but just so you know you have some freedom here on how to handle that rite.

Try not to omit this presentation. I know it's extra work during a busy season of the year, and the liturgy is so short it hardly seems worth the time. But it is.

I try to connect these presentations with some other Lenten event in the parish. You can use them as the opening prayer for an adult education session. You can blend them with the stations of the cross. One year we scheduled the presentation of the creed when the Knights of Columbus had their monthly meeting. They all came over to church and joined us for the liturgy. If you have an evening Mass during Lent, you could include the presentations in the Liturgy of the Word. I try to invite many to these celebrations to keep them from being just another event for catechumens. Especially with the presentation of the creed, it is essential that members of the faithful be on hand for it. I look for an opportunity when people who are gathered already can meet with the elect as they make their final preparations for baptism.

The presentations may be made to the baptized candidates (407). This is also new to the history of the catechumenate. However, the candidates the *RCIA* originally had in mind in that paragraph were those baptized as Catholics who never received further catechesis or celebrated the sacraments of confirmation and Communion. If you have baptized candidates who never got formal instruction on the creed or the Lord's Prayer, you could include them in these presentations. They supply ceremonies that were otherwise omitted in baptismal preparations. The rite of baptism for children includes abbreviated forms of the rites of election, scrutinies, and preparation. It also includes the Lord's Prayer. So the person baptized as an infant who never received further training might make a good candidate for these two presentations. However, if you have people baptized in another Christian denomination with experience reciting the creed and the Lord's Prayer, they do *not* make good candidates for these presentations. It would be insulting to their experience as Christians to hand over to them something that they have long made part of their spiritual lives.

Incidentally, paragraph 407 mentions a third presentation, the one of the Gospels. It appears in the rite of acceptance in paragraphs 61 and 64; see p. 21 and p. 23. It does not share the same historical origins of the other two.

157. The rubrics recommend that you celebrate the presentation of the creed during Mass after the homily. It should take place during the week of the first scrutiny. The elect are thereby purified and made ready to receive the creed. They have reflected on the story of the woman at the well. They believe that Jesus knows them, and now they want to know more about him and to tell others about their experience. The creed will give them words.

This should not take place on a Sunday. Do the scrutinies on Sundays, but the presentations are less important. They belong on weekdays. I often do them in the midst of a word service rather than a Mass. But if the elect can attend one of your regularly scheduled weekday Masses, that would make an ideal setting for this celebration.

158. You may replace the regular weekday readings with those recommended for the presentation of the creed. If done at Mass, this will mean displacing the beautiful readings of a Lenten weekday, but it is for a good cause.

The recommended readings are cited here. You can also find them at #748 in the Lectionary. The selections are magnificently apt. In the first reading, Moses summarizes the Law and presents his creed to the people: "Hear, O Israel, the Lord is our God, the Lord alone. Therefore, you shall love the Lord your God" (Deuteronomy 6:4–5). The psalm blends praise of God's law with the faith-filled words of Peter, addressed to Jesus when other disciples were turning away from him because of the impenetrably demanding doctrine of the Eucharist: "Lord, you have the words of everlasting life" (John 6:68c).

There are two options for the second reading. The first, from Romans, includes a line dear to the heart of many fundamentalist Christians, and one that should be dear to the heart of Catholics as well: "If you confess with your mouth that Jesus is Lord and believe in your heart that God raised him from the dead, you will be saved" (Romans 10:9). The other option comes from First Corinthians, in which Paul hands on what he received as of first importance: the death and resurrection of Jesus Christ. Both these are classic texts at the core of Christian belief, and the implications for holding it.

The verse for the Gospel acclamation is dear to the heart of every Christian: "God so loved the world that he gave his only-begotten Son, so that everyone who believes in him might have eternal life" (John 3.16).

There are two options for the gospel. In the first, Peter makes his confession of faith that Jesus is the Christ, the Son of the living God. In the second, Jesus promises light to all those who believe in him. These are all wonderful passages, and they will give the elect much to ponder.

159. In your homily you explain the selected texts and the importance of the creed to our lives as Christians. You explain to the elect that they will be baptized on the strength of their adherence to the creed, and that they must live by it all the days of their lives.

160. A deacon or another assisting minister invites the elect forward to receive the creed. A catechist could do this as well. The role is given to someone besides you—partly because it is an invitation to people to perform an action, similar to the sign of peace and dismissal at Mass, and partly because this creed belongs to everyone, not just to you.

The elect are asked to "come forward." I often do it differently, though. By this time, the elect have "come forward" a lot—for every special rite and dismissal. Many of them have done so reluctantly, especially if they don't like calling attention to their inner spiritual journey, or if they are not comfortable in front of others. The number of rituals is multiplying. So I give them a break on this and turn the tables. After all, the elect are *receiving* the creed. They are not the agents of this ritual. They are completely passive. Ready for this? I invite the *assembly* into the sanctuary. On a weekday it's usually a small enough group, and it creates a lively atmosphere. With the assembly in the sanctuary, I ask them to present the creed to the few elect who remain in the pews. It's humorous to turn the tables this way, but I think it sends a very important message to the *faithful. We* are the agents of this liturgy. We are the ones handing on the creed. So we occupy the sanctuary to do it.

On most Sundays, we profess our faith as part of our own celebration of the Liturgy of the Eucharist. But on this day, we profess our faith with a more specific intent: we are handing it on to a particular group of people. We speak and they listen.

You address the elect, so they know what is at hand. You may choose your own words, but a sample text is provided.

The faithful may present the Apostles' Creed or the Nicene Creed. Both are valuable treasures in our Church. The elect will be reciting the Nicene Creed nearly every week at Mass, so there is some value to using it here. It's also the one the faithful probably know better. But the Apostles' Creed, in my opinion, makes the better choice. The *Roman Missal* now recommends that the faithful recite the Apostles' Creed on the Sundays of Lent and Easter because of its connection to the baptismal promises. When the elect come to be baptized, they will be asked three questions based more nearly on the Apostles' Creed than on the Nicene. For this reason, I think presenting the Apostles' Creed pulls together the themes of the season of Lent and Easter. It is the creed the assembly will recite on the Sundays surrounding the presentation, and it is the creed more nearly inspired by the baptismal promises of the elect. You may use either one, but I recommend the Apostles' Creed.

By the way, notice that there is no physical presentation of a creed. There is no written document that you hand over to the elect. The liturgy does not ask you to get a nicely framed parchment of the creed inscribed in calligraphy. None of that. There is a cottage industry of printed creeds that you may purchase by credit card and present to the elect. Don't fall for that. Following the ancient tradition, the creed is not something you write down. It is not something you pass from hand to hand. You pass it from mouth to ear, and from heart to heart. It is part of a Christian's being, not an accessory on the wall of one's spiritual life.

161. You invite the faithful to pray for the elect. You may use your own words, but a text is suggested. If I've invited the faithful to the sanctuary, I let them return to their places before this prayer.

All pray in silence. Then you stretch out your hands over the elect and offer a prayer for them. In some parishes the assembly also extends hands.

162. If the presentation takes place during Mass, you dismiss the elect. If this takes place in a word service, you dismiss everyone. All may sing a song.

163. If this took place during Mass, you resume the service. There has been no series of intercessions yet, so the place where you resume Mass is the prayer of the faithful. By this time, it should be clear to the faithful that the prayer "of the faithful" is their prayer—not the prayer of the catechumens. As baptized members of the priestly people of God, they have a responsibility to pray. They exercise it weekly with these petitions.

178. The presentation of the Lord's Prayer is also recommended within Mass, but it may be celebrated as a word service. It takes place during the week of the third scrutiny. However, as indicated above, it may also be celebrated during the period of the catechumenate *prior* to the rite of election or even on Holy Saturday morning as part of the preparation rites. These paragraphs, however, tell you how to do it on a weekday in Lent. It should not take place on a Sunday in Lent. Keep those for the scrutinies. If you are celebrating this during the period of the catechumenate, you might think it more attractive to do it on a Sunday, especially if the Lord's Prayer is already the Gospel of that day. However, inexplicably, Matthew's version of the Lord's Prayer, which is the Gospel for this rite, *never* appears in the Sunday Lectionary. It shows up on Tuesday of the First Week of Lent (225) and Thursday of the Eleventh Week in Ordinary Time (368). Luke's version appears as the Gospel for the Seventeenth Sunday in Ordinary Time Year C (111), a day that shows up in the calendar in the middle of summer. When you incorporate a sacrament such as baptism into Sunday Mass, you may change at least one scripture reading, so you could use that principle to change the Gospel on some other Sunday when you wanted to celebrate this rite. But I think it's usually not a good idea to alter the Sunday cycle of Gospels.

179. The readings for this rite are lovely. The passages are cited in this paragraph, but you may also find them in the Lectionary at #749. The reading from Hosea presents God as a parent taking care of a young child, teaching the kid to walk, and cuddling cheek to cheek. It's arguably a maternal image of God, but it is used as a prelude to Jesus' invitation to Christians to call God by the title "Father."

There are two options for the psalm. The first is everyone's favorite: "The Lord is my shepherd" (Psalm 23:1). Again the scriptures use a very intimate image for God's relationship to the people. God leads us to restful waters, guides us through dark valleys, gives us courage, spreads a feast before us, anoints us with oil. This is no distant God, but one who cares and steers every individual yearning to live in the house of the Lord like a member of the family.

The second option should not be overlooked. It includes this evocative refrain: "As a father is kind to his children, so kind is the Lord to those who fear him" (Psalm 103:13). That refrain is filled with implications for human fathers, as well as interpretations of how God cares for us. But the overwhelming image is that God is the sort of father who is kind; people fear him, so there must be some awareness that even a kind dad may reprove wrongdoing. Still, at the end of the day, God is kind, not punishing.

A practical caution: If a reader is going to read the second version of this psalm, you may want to give people the text of their refrain in print. It's too cumbersome to remember upon hearing it once.

There are two options for the second reading. In both passages Paul permits Christians to call God "Abba"—that is, "Father." The verse before the Gospel quotes the first option of these readings.

180. The Gospel will be the Lord's Prayer from Matthew, the version we all know. Luke's version is shorter, and some scholars think it is therefore the earlier version. It's easier to see how Matthew could have added a couple of lines than to explain why Luke would have struck them. But Matthew's version is the one quoted in a turn-of-the-first-century catechetical manual called the *Didache*, and it has stayed with us as the more popular version. No complaints here.

The deacon or another minister invites the elect forward to receive the Lord's Prayer. As in the presentation of the creed, you do not do this. Someone else does. If you have no deacon a catechist may do it. The Lord's Prayer belongs to all of us, so another member of the faithful may extend the invitation.

I usually gather the elect right in front of the ambo and have them face me. They are to receive the Lord's Prayer, and they are going to hear it from the proclamation of the Gospel. I want them close to the word of God.

You ask them to listen to the reading. You may use your own words, but a sample text is provided. If you use the sample text, you'll need to have the *RCIA* at the ambo. It looks cleaner if you leave the book behind and use your own words.

You proclaim the Gospel. *You* do this. The *RCIA* does not have the deacon proclaim this Gospel. Even when the bishop presides, a deacon invites the elect forward, but the bishop proclaims this Gospel (*CB* 72). This probably indicates that the priest is the one who presides over the presentations, and his role supersedes a normal function of the deacon in this single instance.

The rubrics do not indicate that you start with a greeting and end with an acclamation, but logically you would treat this Gospel the same way you treat any that appear during Mass. Bow to the altar on your way to the ambo. Ask the elect to listen to the reading. Greet the people ("The Lord be with you.") Announce the citation ("A reading from the holy Gospel . . ."). Use incense if you wish. Proclaim the text, and conclude with the acclamation and response ("The Gospel of the Lord").

As with the presentation of the creed, note that there is no handing on of a printed text. The elect receive the Gospel in its proclamation. When the readings are proclaimed in any liturgy, God is speaking to us. When you or the deacon proclaim the Gospel, Christ is present, speaking (*GIRM* 55, 60). The elect receive the Lord's Prayer the same way the disciples did: from the voice of Jesus. The "presentation" of the Lord's Prayer is not the handing over of paper; it is Christ speaking to disciples, telling them aloud how to pray.

181. You deliver a homily about the importance of the Lord's Prayer. You should be able to speak from a lot of experience on this theme.

182. You invite everyone to pray for the elect. You may use your own words, but a sample text is provided. Then you extend your hands over the group and offer the prayer.

183. You dismiss the elect. If this is a word service, you dismiss everyone. If this takes place at Mass, you dismiss the elect and then proceed with the rest of the service. You start with the prayer of the faithful. Mass will include the Lord's Prayer, and it should alert the faithful to the significance of this prayer as part of their preparation for Communion.

```
┌─────────────────────────────────┐
│  ┌───────────────────────────┐  │
│  │                           │  │
│  │     Preparation Rites     │  │
│  │      (RCIA 193–205)       │  │
│  │                           │  │
│  └───────────────────────────┘  │
└─────────────────────────────────┘
```

Preparation Rites (RCIA 193–205)

Sometime before the Vigil on Holy Saturday you celebrate the preparation rites for those who will be baptized that night. These lack the status of the rites of acceptance and election, which mark stages in the catechumenate, and of the scrutinies, which take place during Sunday Mass, but they form the prelude to baptism. Think of them not as the end of the period of purification and enlightenment, but as the beginning of the rites of baptism. The rubrics do not designate the color for your stole, but I choose white, not violet. Lent is over, and this liturgy begins the celebration of baptism.

These rites "may be celebrated" especially if the elect are coming together on Holy Saturday for reflection and prayer (185/2). The *RCIA* does not command you to do these, but I think they are important, especially the return of the creed.

I schedule the preparation rites on Holy Saturday morning, and I realize this is not the most carefree day of the year. The decorators need access to the church. Readers and servers need rehearsals. You have homilies to prepare, you have the very complicated Easter Vigil coming up, and you probably want to cram the flow of the liturgy into your head before lighting the fire. Holy Saturday is busy, but these are important rites because they establish a tone for the day, and they set the stage for baptism. Make time for them.

Oddly, the rubrics never indicate that anyone else is present except you and the elect. This must be an oversight. I invite the parish to these rites. Every parish has a core group coming to daily Mass, and they may participate in this prayer. It shouldn't look like a private ceremony, especially because it includes the return of the creed. Just as representatives of the community need to be on hand for the presentation of the creed, so should some receive it back from the elect. I don't have unreasonable expectations about attendance at this event, but I do invite the parish to come.

Every so often the liturgical books do not give you all the information you need, or they arrange it in a way that is not very helpful. The preparation rites of Holy Saturday are an annoying example. The texts you need are scattered through several different books. The elements of this liturgy are straightforward, but I always have to prepare a cue sheet to remember what follows what and where to find it.

Infants may complicate matters further.

◆ The Church recommends conducting infant baptism during the Easter Vigil (*RBC* 9, 28). It's a great idea, really, and the third edition of the *Roman Missal* now explains more fully how this is done. There is an ancient tradition behind baptizing adults and infants at the Easter liturgy. Offering baptism when the Church celebrates the resurrection helps explicate its meaning. There are practical problems in bringing infants to the Vigil, but the idea is a good one, and some families will find it appealing.

◆ Certain elements of infant baptism are supposed to take place earlier in the day—not during the Vigil (*RBC* 28/1). Whereas the preparation rites for adults "may be celebrated," the preliminary part of baptizing infants "is celebrated." You really should do it. The most logical occasion for it is the preparation rites for the elect. You could schedule the infants separately, but one liturgy can fittingly gather all the missing and anticipatory elements of baptism. The rubrics do not tell you how to do it, so you have to use some of your own wisdom. I've placed a diamond before some comments in this section to help you with infants.

The preparation rites are for the unbaptized. They are prebaptismal elements. Do not ask baptized candidates to undergo prebaptismal rites.

The *RCIA* seems to presume a priest will preside. You could argue that a deacon may do it; after all, deacons may conduct baptism, so they are certainly competent for its ancillary rites. However, these particular ones are preliminary to the baptisms at the Vigil. The preparation rites will have more integrity if the person who baptizes begins the day by presiding over them. That person is you.

You'll need some help: someone to lead the singing, a sacristan to set up the right books, a reader, a server, the godparents, the catechists. There's quite a bit going on.

For an outline of the preparation rites, see *RCIA* 187–192. The next paragraphs contain the rites, but not all of them, and not in the proper sequence. Good luck.

187. Open with a song. If you can get a cantor or some musicians on hand, that'd be great. No text is recommended, but a psalm such as 42 ("My soul is thirsting") or a number from the baptism section of your parish's hymnal would make a good choice.

◆ If you have infants, start at the door. Otherwise, begin at your chair with the people in the nave. The adults already had their ritual at the door in the rite of acceptance.

188. You greet the people. There is no call for the sign of the cross. This is not Mass, so the liturgy doesn't begin the same way. You may use one of the traditional greetings, such as "The Lord be with you," but you may use other words of welcome too. I think a traditional greeting sets the right tone, and it can be followed by other words of explanation.

If you have infants, note the following:

◆ This would be the logical time to lead the reception of them at the door (*RBC* 28/1, and 37–41). After the greeting, you ask for the names of the infants. If you want to do something more with the baptismal name of infants and adults, see the comments on *RCIA* 200–202 below (p. 99). You could move that part of the liturgy forward to this point.

◆ You ascertain the intentions of the parents and godparents. You sign the infants with the cross. You do not sign the adults; you did that already in the rite of acceptance.

◆ You process into the church and take your places in the sanctuary and the nave.

The rubrics make no mention of a collect. I like to include one here, but none is supplied and no provision for it appears in the outline of the preparation rites. The most logical one to use is the one for Holy Saturday from the Liturgy of the Hours. But, of course, you'll need to have *that* book handy if you want to use it. You could also improvise a prayer, praising God for calling these individuals to the waters of baptism and praying that they will celebrate the rites worthily and well. It's not in the rubrics, but I don't think God will punish us for saying an extra prayer.

189. The Liturgy of the Word comes next. You have an embarrassment of riches here. You may choose texts from among the following:

• The presentation of the Lord's Prayer requires the proclamation of the pertinent passage from Matthew (*LM* 749; *RCIA* 179 and 180; see p. 89 above for comments).

• The ephphetha rite suggests the Gospel from which it derives (198). You can find the text on Sunday of the Twenty-third Week in Ordinary Time, Year B (*LM* 128) and on Friday of the Fifth Week in Ordinary Time (*LM* 333).

• The recitation of the creed (194) offers you two options for a Gospel; the first is nearly identical to the first choice for the presentation of the creed, and the second is the full text of the passage excerpted as the refrain to the responsorial psalm from the same rite (158). In both stories Peter professes his faith in Jesus. You can find the first option at *LM* 121 (Twenty-first Sunday in Ordinary Time, Year A), if you omit the last few verses. The second option does not appear in the Lectionary, but parts of it are at 274 and 278 (Tuesday and Saturday of the Third Week of Easter). See a Bible for the full text.

• For choosing the baptismal name, *RCIA* 201 offers a selection of texts in which biblical figures are given new names. The recommended passages from Genesis and Revelation are not in the Lectionary; use a Bible. The passage from Isaiah appears as the first reading of the Christmas Vigil (*LM* 13) and for the Second Sunday in Ordinary Time, Year C (66). The one from Matthew can be culled from the Twenty-first Sunday in Ordinary Time, Year A (121). The one from John is an abbreviation of the Gospel for the Second Sunday in Ordinary Time, Year B (65) or the one for January 4 (207).

The result should resemble a Liturgy of the Word: choose a first reading, a psalm, a second reading, and a Gospel. You could eliminate the second reading; in fact you could eliminate everything except the gospel. But hearing more than one passage will make this feel more like a liturgical celebration for those now familiar with this format. You don't have to pick one reading from each of the rites you are going to celebrate.

However, 194 says that after the Gospel and homily for the recitation of the creed, you may read the Gospel for the ephphetha and preach on it. I can't believe the *RCIA* really means that. One Gospel and one homily should suffice. It probably means you conduct the rite without the extra reading and homily.

If you include the presentation of the Lord's Prayer, that Gospel will trump the use of any other (180). I find it simplest to choose all the scriptures from the presentation of the Lord's Prayer, but if you are celebrating that rite at some other time, you open up several other possibilities for this Saturday's readings.

I recommend presenting the Lord's Prayer on Holy Saturday for several reasons. As I mentioned above (p. 83), this presentation has a different context than the presentation of the creed. The one for the creed is to follow the first scrutiny, and this one follows the third. There are precedents for this sequence of events in the first centuries of Christianity. The elect get the creed as soon as possible after they are first scrutinized, so that it may serve as part of their proximate preparation for baptism. The presentation of the Lord's Prayer occurs later, after the scrutinies are completed. It is less part of the catechetical preparation for baptism and more part of the spiritual preparation for the Eucharist. All of us pray the Lord's Prayer together each time we receive Communion. The elect will, too, after they are baptized during the Easter Vigil. But first we give it to them. The presentation of this prayer comes in close proximity to their First Communion. Among the early Church Fathers commenting on the presentation of the Lord's Prayer is St. Augustine (+403), who explicitly says it was done on Holy Saturday morning. That is why we have this option today: If it was good enough for Augustine, it's good enough for us.

But I have another practical, even selfish reason for doing the presentation of the Lord's Prayer on Holy Saturday morning: It's one less thing to do during the fifth week of Lent. In a busy parish it is hard to schedule another event so close to Easter, especially if it means giving up all or part of an evening. Lent brings its share of extras in parish life, from adult catechesis to penance services. It's not just me, but the elect themselves and the catechumenate team appreciate knowing they don't have to rearrange their schedules for an extra prayer service so close to Easter.

190. You preach a homily that explains the readings and the ceremonies that are unfolding. Keep it brief, but make it meaningful. Help people reflect already on the significant events to come. Incidentally, *RCIA* 198 calls this an "instruction," but the word in Latin is the same. It's a homily.

191. Choose from the rites the ones you will use. If you are going to celebrate the ephphetha, it comes next.

197. The word comes from the story of Jesus curing a deaf man with a speech impediment. It is spelled "ephphatha" in the Gospel and "ephphetha" in the *RCIA* and *RBC*.

199. The elect come up to you, though the *RCIA* never says how they get there. You may invite them, or their godparents may escort them, or a deacon or catechist may make the request. I usually have the elect stand in the sanctuary facing the assembly.

A song may be sung. No theme is recommended, but a good choice would be something inspired by this Gospel, or that promotes listening to God's word or announcing it to others. Still, you are going to be reciting an important text, and you will want at least the elect, if not the assembly, to hear it. If you have only a few elect, you will probably skip the song. But if you have many, you may want the song to begin after you've recited the text aloud a couple of times, so everyone knows what is going on before they sing.

With your thumb you touch the right and left ear and the closed lips of each of the elect, while you say the formula. When Jesus performed this miracle, he put his fingers into the man's ears and touched his tongue with spittle. Don't try this at home. Some priests trace a cross with their thumb, but the rite does not call for that. It just says you touch the ears and lips.

Even in Latin the text doesn't line up exactly with your actions. The rubrics call for you to touch the ears and then the lips, whereas the text mentions professing and then hearing. Logically, the elect hear before they profess, so that explains the sequence of touches. In fact, the English translation says "that you may profess the faith you hear," whereas the Latin says "that you may profess the faith you *have heard*." It's not a big deal, but it makes a little more sense that way. Don't be concerned about trying to connect your touch too literally with the text.

Or try this: Close the person's ears with the palms of your hands—or with your thumbs—while you say the word, "Ephphetha." Then release as you give the translation in English: "Be opened." Then press lightly on the person's lower lip, as you pray that they will profess the faith they hear. Someone will have to hold the book for you if need to see the text.

Other priests or deacons may assist you if you have many elect. You each touch the ears and lips of some of the elect. Each of you should say the formula each time. Don't say the formula once and then go down the line touching faces. The words and actions go together.

◆If you have children to be baptized, you could include them in the ephpheta you conduct for the adults. In the *RBC* the ephpheta *follows* baptism (65–66), but in the *RCIA* it *precedes* baptism. The rite is optional for children, so it may be omitted. In fact, the Third Edition of the *Roman Missal* says you do omit the ephpheta for children (51). But it is speaking about the Vigil. In my opinion, you could fittingly include it here if children are included in the prebaptismal ceremonies for adults.

193. The recitation of the creed is a highlight of these preparation rites. It complements the presentation of the creed, which took place earlier (p. 82). The connection between these two rituals is easier to catch in their Latin titles. The one we call the "presentation" is the *traditio*, and the one we call the "recitation" is the *redditio*. One is a handing on of the creed, and the other is its return. The faithful announce it to the elect, and the elect recite it back. St. Augustine said catechumens were expected to return the creed in person directly to the bishop—from memory. If they could not, the bishop had the option of postponing their baptism. We don't do it that way any more. Still, the elect should meditate deeply on the creed in the weeks before Easter.

If for some reason you never presented the creed, the recitation of the creed is not celebrated (186/1). But surely one should avoid this circumstance. Returning the creed prepares the elect for the impending moment at the Vigil when they will profess the faith in response to your questions just before they are baptized. All through Lent, we have prayed the scrutinies for these people, asking God to purge what is evil and to strengthen what is good. On Holy Saturday we learn how effective this has been. The elect will return our creed, and we will tell by their proclamation if they are holding it in their heart.

195. The Latin original of the *RCIA* permits you to anoint the elect either before the return of the creed to prepare for it, or afterward to confirm it (*Ordo initiationis Christianae adultorum 206*). The *Roman Missal* instructs you to anoint them during the baptisms at the Easter Vigil. (I'll get to this on p. 108) unless you did it at the preparation rites. However, in the United States the anointing at the preparation rites and at the Vigil was suppressed (*RCIA* 33/7, NS 16). Although it appears that the *Roman Missal* has reinstated it, the local legislation still stands. You may anoint with the oil of catechumens on more than one occasion (100), but it should be done during the period of the catechumenate, not on Holy Saturday.

For the prayer before the recitation, you stretch your hands out over the elect and say a prayer for them. I would want the elect in the sanctuary for this. If you have performed the ephphetha, they are already there. If not, they would appropriately come up to you before you pray for them. You could let them remain in their places in the nave, but their role in this liturgy will be less visible.

196. The elect recite the creed, preferably from the sanctuary. Now they are the agents of this rite. We need to hear the faith from them. They use either the Apostles' or the Nicene Creed, depending on which one they received in the presentation of the creed. As I explained above (p. 87), I prefer the Apostles' Creed for this because of its direct connection with the questions that immediately precede baptism, but you are free to choose either one.

It would be great if the elect had this memorized. Most of them are too nervous and too distracted on this day. The text is long and dense. Memorization may be difficult for them to achieve. But I can think of no better spiritual preparation for them during the weeks before their baptism than to commit the creed to memory. If they can say it from memory to the community, we have a clear indication how much these words mean to them. But I never require it. If they want to read it from a printed aid, I let them.

You may anoint with the oil of catechumens after the creed instead of before it. See 195 on p. 98 above.

200–202. The optional ceremony about the baptismal name comes next, but see my comments about 189 on p. 95 above. Remember, in the United States the elect do not choose a new name for their baptism (33/4). However, an explanation of their given name may be made if the elect are not too numerous.

202B. After hearing the name of the elect, you may connect it to Christian values or cite a text from the Bible that relates to the person's name.

I have done this: I have asked each of the elect to explain during this ceremony why they have the name they have. Parents of the infants get the same question. The group is usually small enough for this kind of sharing. If necessary, I have them use a microphone. My question is this: How did your parents decide on your name? Were you named after someone else in the family? A movie star? A favorite saint? Some of these stories reveal family values. Sometimes the family expresses its hopes for the future of the child by the choice of the name; other times they just want something that sounds good. In any case, we learn something about the heritage of those to be baptized. I apply some Christian interpretation to this.

203. You conclude the celebration with prayer, announcements, and a dismissal. If the elect have entered the sanctuary for the preparation rites, they could return to their places before you lead these concluding elements. However, even these final words are mostly directed to the elect, so you could keep them in place. Still, the liturgy will have more finality if people go back to the nave.

204. You stretch out your hands and offer another prayer over the elect. This one helps them prepare for their baptism. The previous prayer helped prepare them to recite the creed. Note there is no list of intercessions here—just a prayer of blessing.

205. You make announcements. Remind the elect where and when to come for the Vigil. Encourage them to spend the day in prayer and fasting as much as possible, and to refrain from their usual activities (22, 185). In fact, all members of the community are urged to fast on Holy Saturday, just as they do on Good Friday (*General Norms for the Liturgical Year and Calendar*, 20; *Sacrosanctum concilium* 110). Most Catholic calendars print a purple fish on Good Friday because that is a canonical day of fast and abstinence (*CCL* 1251), but none of them puts even a perforated fish up there for Holy Saturday. According to a custom dating back to the turn of the second century, the entire community is urged to fast on Holy Saturday in solidarity with those who are to be baptized. This differs from the penitential fast of Ash Wednesday and Good Friday. It is a fast of hungry anticipation for meeting Christ in the waters of baptism. The net result is the same—don't eat too much. But the purpose is different: Easter is nearly here.

The rubrics say you make the announcements, but traditionally anyone may do this. If it makes more sense for a catechist or the director of the catechumenate to give these instructions, let him or her do so.

You dismiss the group. A formula is given, but you may choose another one. The elect are supposed to answer, "Amen," but no one will know this without a rehearsal or a participation aid. It isn't that important. If they know a concluding formula such as "Go in peace," to which they answer "Thanks be to God," it will be fine.

Celebration of the Sacraments of Initiation (Easter Vigil) (RCIA 218–243)

St. Augustine once called the Easter Vigil the mother of all vigils. He meant the source and inspiration of all other vigils, not the most horrendous of all vigils. For most priests, this is the most complicated liturgy of the year, and it requires much mental preparation. During the day, the presider needs to take time with the liturgical books to recall what follows what, and which cues trigger certain events. From fire to water, from word to Eucharist, no other liturgy demands as much from us as the Easter Vigil.

And with good reason. Everything we are and do hinges on this night. On this night Christ rises in our community and in our hearts. On this night we profess our faith in the Resurrection. We greet the risen Christ in fire, word, and sacrament. It is the most important celebration of the Christian year. Many people avoid it because it is long. But they are missing out on the single most important opportunity to renew and celebrate their faith in the Resurrection, which gives hope and direction all our days.

This book is about the initiation rites, not about the Vigil, but I want to encourage you to use big symbols not just when baptizing but throughout the entire Vigil. Give initiation a proper context. Arrange for a sizeable fire outside the church. Gather people there before the liturgy begins. Use all the readings. Yes, all nine of them. The *Roman Missal* encourages this practice, but most parishes trim the readings down. The Vigil is not a time to cut corners, and the readings, responses, and prayers make this Vigil a vigil. Some presiders promise people a ninety-minute vigil, as if this is desirable. It's not. One of the symbols of the Vigil is its length. This is counter-cultural, but Christians should not want to be anywhere else besides church on Holy Saturday night, and not be in a hurry to go anywhere else once they are there. If they put aside their expectations about length, they will receive the grace of letting the Vigil wash over them in all its grandness. The Eucharist will feel like a real climax to all the proceedings.

Offer a reception afterward. Start the liturgy late, and end it late. There is nothing quite like it, and it has the power of anchoring the spiritual life of the faithful for the year to come.

Incidentally, you may begin the Vigil in the wee hours of the morning if you prefer. Some communities start it at 3:00 or 4:00 a.m. on Sunday, rather than at 8 or 9 p.m. on Saturday. The entire Vigil is supposed to take place in the dark. The Sunday morning option has some advantages. It makes Saturday a real day in the tomb with Christ. If you are fasting on Saturday as well as on Good Friday, you will especially feel the emptiness of this day. Starting on Sunday morning also ends the Vigil with dawn, early in the morning on the first day of the week, the time and day when the Gospel women discovered the Resurrection.

However, if you and the choir have more Easter liturgies to celebrate on Sunday morning, this may not be appealing at all. You'll be exhausted after an early morning Vigil, and it will be hard to summon the energy to lead the faithful through more Easter Masses in the next few hours. Besides, attendance might be even worse early Sunday morning than it is late Saturday night. I've had parishioners tell me that if I start the vigil at 3:00 a.m., I'll be the only one there. Still, know that you have options.

The heading of this section of the *RCIA* has the words Easter Vigil in parentheses because it is permissible (though not advisable) to baptize adults on other occasions. This is the rite of adult baptism no matter when you observe it. But the Easter Vigil is the best occasion.

The design of the Easter Vigil is that it will include baptisms. The design is not that it will include the rite of reception for previously baptized Christians, but quite a number of parishes combine the rites and offer them at the Vigil.

The rite of reception may be celebrated at any time of year. It is not reserved to Easter. When the English translation of the *RCIA* was being prepared, a combined rite of baptism and reception was included in its appendix, and that is the one many parishes use. However, Rome was hesitant to permit the combined rite at all because it would threaten to cloud our teaching about the validity of baptisms in other Christian churches. That is why the combined rites appear in an appendix. Rome was hoping that few people would notice them there, or that all would realize that the combined rites were a second-class solution to the liturgical need. Putting them in the appendix, though, didn't make any difference. People use them.

If you separate the rite of reception from the Vigil, you accomplish some very positive goals. You allow other validly baptized Christians to be received into the full communion of the Catholic Church whenever they are ready at any time of year. And you preserve the symbolic integrity of the Easter Vigil, which upholds baptism as one of the primary signs of the Resurrection.

Flip to the back of the *RCIA* and look up National Statutes #33. It says it is preferable *not* to celebrate the rite of reception at the Easter Vigil. You may do it, but it is not ideal.

First, let's look at how the Easter Vigil goes without the rite of reception, and then we'll take a look at the combined rite. If you have no baptisms at all, you could celebrate the rite of reception at the Easter Vigil, but that is not particularly advantageous. The ideal time to receive a baptized person into the Church is when he or she is ready, not just when Easter rolls around.

If you are going to step into the water and baptize by immersion, dress accordingly before you vest. For example, wear gym shorts under your pants, or wear sweat pants that you can hike up your legs before entering the water. Be sure your elect are dressed accordingly as well. They can wear whatever they don't mind getting wet, and they may don a loose-fitting garment over it for decorum. If this garment is off-white, beige, yellow, or some neutral color that is not white, it will contrast with the white garment after baptism.

The Missal's presentation of the Easter Vigil does not include the full liturgy of baptism. When you get to this part of the Mass, you put the Missal aside and take up the *RCIA*, which contains the additional rubrics and texts for baptism and confirmation. (Some priests preside with texts copied into a specially prepared binder, in spite of copyright issues.) You switch books after you bless the font and the people make their acclamation (Missal 47).

218 [Missal 37]. Baptism takes place after the homily. If your font is in full view of the faithful, baptize there. If it is not, you may set up a vessel of water in the sanctuary. You could also set up a font somewhere else; for example, at the doors, in the aisle, or at the crossing. The primary concern of this paragraph is visibility.

Many of our churches were built prior to the more public celebrations of baptism. The font occupied an area in a side chapel, often large enough for only a few people to gather. The very architecture of our churches made baptism a private event.

Newer churches have taken a different approach. Many of them fan the seating around the altar and the entrance, so that a font can be located near the door of the church where it serves as the holy water stoup, and where it is fully visible to everyone for the baptismal rites.

Some older churches have been retrofitted. Sometimes it works; sometimes it does not. If you get into a fight with a building, the building usually wins. Some churches are just not adaptable to modern liturgical needs. If there is no logical solution to locating a font permanently in a visible space, some long-term solutions should be considered, including the redesign or replacement of the entire church.

Some parishes have institutionalized the temporary nature of their font. They have one on wheels stored in a closet to be retrieved in case of baptism. This sends an unfortunate catechetical message: that baptism is not very important, that it should be tucked away most days.

If you are using a temporary font for the Vigil, that should be your first clue that another solution needs to be planned for some time in the future.

219 [Missal 38-39]. Someone presents the candidates for baptism. In print this looks more complicated than it really is. Options A, B, and C cover these circumstances respectively: a font close at hand, a font requiring a procession to get there, and a temporary font in the sanctuary; all three have other options depending on the size of the group. The point is to move the elect from their places in the nave to the place where they will be baptized. If the group is not too numerous, someone should announce the names of the elect. Honestly, though, even with a large group it would be good to announce names at this time.

Whoever introduces the elect should know how to pronounce their names. A deacon or catechist who has had contact with the group usually does this well. This person should stand near a microphone, but not at the ambo.

220 [Missal 40]. You introduce the litany of the saints. You may use your own words. Your introduction should urge people to join in prayer, and it serves as a cue to the cantors to start singing.

221 [Missal 41, 43]. The litany is sung. Ideally, this is the music that covers the procession—however long or short it may be.

You may include other saints—for example, the patrons of your parish, the city, the diocese, or of the elect. To finesse this, your cantors could insert these additional patrons into the proper slot. The litany opens with Mary and the angels, and then addresses biblical figures, early martyrs (male and female), theologians, monks and founders of religious communities, more recent patrons and doctors of the church. The litany moves chronologically. You don't have to do this, but if your patron is Anne, for example, she probably belongs right before John the Baptist. Thomas Aquinas would appear right after Francis and Dominic. And so on.

You may also add petitions suitable to the occasion. The litany has plenty of intentions, but if you have some specific things requiring God's help (plague, inclement weather, war), you would insert those near the end among the brief phrases that call for the response, "Lord, hear our prayer."

If you are going to step into the water for baptisms by immersion, this is a good time to remove your chasuble, shoes, and socks. If you've been wearing a wireless microphone, you may want to take it off, too.

Godparents should accompany the elect to the place where they will be baptized. It looks good if they lead them there, even placing a hand on their shoulder or around their waist—whatever looks and feels natural.

When you get to the font, you want everyone to be able to see and hear what is going on. The elect and their godparents should be arranged in a way that does not block the view of the assembly.

In the Missal, the litany of the saints concludes with a prayer ("Almighty and ever-living God, be present by the mysteries of your great love . . .") This prayer was omitted in the *RCIA*. The English translation is not at fault. The prayer was omitted from the Latin original. If you have been using the Missal—not the *RCIA*—up to this point, you have no problem. The text is right there.

222 [Missal 44-47]. You bless the water. This is an ancient tradition in the Church, and the imagery of this prayer is rich, but it is lengthy and hard for some people to follow. There are several options for the water blessing, but you're supposed to use the first—Option A—at the Easter Vigil and that is the only one that appears in the Missal. I think this prayer would have been rendered more pastorally effective if it had been punctuated with acclamations by the people in the style of options B and C.

You face the water. You may sing or recite the blessing. The 1988 Circular Letter from the Congregation for Divine Worship, *Paschale solemnitatis,* encourages you to sing it (42). Singing should lend more dignity to it. The chant appears in the Missal, and it is not too difficult to master. You may find other settings from various music publishers.

Just before the end of the prayer you may lower the Easter candle into the water once or three times—or not at all. Hold it there until everyone has sung the acclamation that follows the blessing. Much psycho-sexual typology has been applied to this action—the phallic candle impregnating the pool of water, rendering it fertile. It is hard to ignore once you think about it, but the action more nearly resembles an *epiclesis*. Apart from the Easter Vigil, instead of lowering the candle you touch the water with your right hand as you bless it; see p. 148. No one claims that is a fertility symbol. You are asking God to send the Spirit upon the water through the intercession of Christ our Lord.

The rubrics say you lower the candle if "appropriate." It always seems unwieldy, but always appropriate. Because the rubrics give some leeway, I often ask a deacon or server to move the candle into position for me, so that I can stay focused on the text.

The rubrics in the Missal now say to hold your hands in the *orans* position. This was left unclear in the RCIA.

People should sing "Amen" when you conclude the prayer, and then they add their acclamation, "Springs of water, bless the Lord." Just be sure the musicians know what the cues are.

Options B and C are for blessing water apart from the Easter Vigil. In B you touch the water with your right hand; in C you make the sign of the cross over it. Options D and E presume you are baptizing shortly after Easter Day with water previously blessed at the Vigil. But at the Vigil, use option A.

None of these additional options is indicated in the combined rite (570) because it is designed exclusively for the Easter Vigil, not for other times of the year.

At the Vigil, it is best to use the *Roman Missal* up to this point. Now, though, you will need the RCIA. Switch books.

223 [Missal 48]. You begin the profession of faith, which also includes the renunciation of sin. If I am baptizing by immersion in a spacious font, I walk into the water right after the blessing, and I help the first of the elect into the water for his or her renunciation and profession. I repeat this with each one. It lengthens their time in the pool and forms a suitable prelude to the act of baptizing. But you could question them outside the font and then step in.

These questions bring the entire period of formation to a head, especially the period of purification and enlightenment. Throughout Lent the elect have undergone scrutinies to expel evil from their hearts and to infuse them with the Holy Spirit. In these moments, the community witnesses the effect of these scrutinies. The elect are asked point blank if they renounce what is evil and believe what is good. Once they do, into the waters they go.

224. For the renunciation of sin, you have several options. Options A and C are probably familiar to you from the *Rite of Baptism for Children* (57). Option B combines the three renunciations into one question, which is also done in the *Rite of Confirmation* (40). You may ask the entire group of the elect to make the renunciations together. I usually ask them to do this individually, but you may do it as a group, especially if the number is large.

If you ask the elect individually for their renunciations, you may obtain their names from their godparents. You really should know their names by now, but if there is any doubt, ask. It's better than baptizing someone with the wrong name.

The rubrics allow you to call each person by name, ask each one for the renunciations, and then proceed back through the entire group asking for the professions of faith. It doesn't make as much sense to me as treating each of them individually with this sequence as a unit: renunciation, profession, and then baptism.

The diocesan bishop may call for specific formularies of renunciation. If drug abuse, pornography, or sectarian violence is rampant, for example, the local ordinary may ask potential new members of the body of Christ to renounce such practices.

The *Roman Missal* has added something here that does not appear in the 1988 *RCIA*. After the elect make their renunciations, they are to be anointed with the oil of catechumens if this was not done in the preparation rites of Holy Saturday; see p. 98. In this context the oil of catechumens acts as a final, protective seal. Now that the candidate for baptism has rejected evil, the oil is applied to help keep it out. This instruction appeared in the 1972 Latin original of the *RCIA*, but it was eliminated from the practice in the United States. This local legislation remains in force, and the anointing does not take place at this time.

225 [Missal 49]. The profession of faith may be made individually or as a group by all those seeking to be baptized. The group option applies to "a great many," which implies extraordinary missionary conditions where the priest baptizes by the hundreds. According to the 2002 *Roman Missal*, facing the same circumstance, you may even have the entire assembly renew its baptismal promises at this time; see 238–239 below. In your parish it is far better to have people respond individually to show the personal decision each has made, and to have the assembly renew its promises later. Again, if baptisms are by immersion, I like to have the elect in the water for these questions.

226 [Missal 50]. You baptize the elect by immersion or pouring (cf. 213). Immersion is listed first because it is the preferred method. See "Christian Initiation: General Introduction" in the front of the *RCIA* (22), the *Catechism of the Catholic Church* (1239), and *NS* 17. Immersion is more common in the Eastern Rites, but it is becoming more popular among Roman Catholics as well. Many priests are skittish about trying it, but many more have zealously embraced it once they have done it and witnessed the reactions of the newly baptized and the community.

When baptizing by immersion, "the whole body" or "the head only" may be immersed. What is the immersion of the head? Beats me. I suspect it's a way to "immerse" someone when the font is no bigger than a soup tureen. In any case, you immerse three times while pronouncing the baptismal formula.

I usually ask the elect to kneel down in the water, and then I bring them face forward three times as I mention the Persons of the Trinity in the baptismal formula. In some Christian traditions, the minister baptizes by lowering the person *backwards* into the font. You may do this, but Catholic fonts are usually rather shallow. Backwards immersions are easier to maneuver if you are up to your armpits in water. But unless you were born on the planet Krypton, you won't have the muscles for a backwards immersion when you are in water up to your knee.

Some immersion fonts are narrow troughs. You stand on dry ground while you immerse the one being baptized.

In some parishes, the priest invites the person to kneel in the water, and then pours water over that person's head. This is also valid, but I think that falls into the category of baptism by pouring, rather than baptism by immersion. In immersion, you bring the person to the water; in pouring you bring the water to the person. Both are valid. Immersion is more expressive.

During an immersion the godparent is supposed to touch the one being baptized; during a pouring the godparent is to place his or her right hand on the shoulder of the one being baptized. If you stand outside a trough-font while immersing someone in the water, the godparent can probably touch the person from the other side. In larger fonts, the only way a sponsor can touch the one being immersed is to enter the water too. There's nothing wrong with this, but it may get crowded in there. More logically, the godparent will be the one to receive the newly baptized as he or she steps from the font.

Each baptism may be followed by a short acclamation. This gives the people a way to rejoice each time. Some communities may burst into spontaneous applause with each baptism, but a sung acclamation can work rather well.

If the group of those to be baptized is very large, other deacons and priests may assist you. Each one has to recite the formula of baptism for each of the elect. The community may spend time singing, listening to scripture, or praying in silence. Ordinarily, though, you'll want the entire community focused on each one being baptized, while responding in some appropriate way.

When baptizing by pouring, the candidate bows his or her head and you pour water three times while you say the formula, once at each mention of a Person of the Trinity. Traditionally you use a utensil resembling a shell to pour water. For a more dramatic effect some ministers pour from a pitcher. Just be careful the result doesn't resemble a locker room victory celebration. Some use a real shell instead. I often simplify it by pouring with the cup of my hand.

227 [Missal 51]. The unhappily named "explanatory rites" follow. They are more expressive, effusive, and evocative than they are explanatory, but whatever you call them, they come next.

228. The Christological anointing on the crown of the head is in brackets. Ordinarily you will not perform this anointing. Shortly you will confirm the adults and children of catechetical age whom you have just baptized. The only ones who receive this anointing are infants you may baptize at the Vigil.

It is unfortunate, in a way, because the text is so expressive, and this anointing has a different meaning than the one that comes later in confirmation. But the framers of the modern catechumenate thought that the two anointings would resemble each other too closely, and that it was better to omit the first.

If you use it, first you recite the text, and then you anoint the newly baptized infant on the crown of the head. I usually pour a tablespoon or more of chrism into the cup of my hand and smear the entire crown of the child's head with it, gently rubbing it around. Then I wipe my hand on a towel provided by an altar server.

229. The newly baptized receive a garment. It should be white or "a color that conforms to local custom." The color white has a lot of tradition in its favor, as well as many scripture passages that speak of it as the color worn by heavenly beings. So to wear a white garment is to show that one already participates in the promised life of heaven. But the rubrics permit another color if that seems better.

The *RCIA* lets you omit this, but the Missal presumes you include it. Ideally, you give the newly baptized the garments that they will wear for the rest of the service. If you are baptizing infants, it makes more sense for the infants to come to church wearing something else, and to receive their fancy baptismal gown at this point; see p. 152. The newly baptized adults may receive an alb they will wear for the rest of the evening. Especially if they have been immersed, the significance of the white garment will be plain.

I avoid those white bibs and stoles that are mass-produced for Catholic baptisms. They don't resemble anything that anyone wears for a formal occasion. Stoles identify ordained clergy; bibs catch drool. Granted, most adults don't walk around in albs, but they do when ministering at the altar at church. I think a full-length garment best expresses one's new life in Christ.

The text invites the newly baptized to "receive" the garment. I usually do *not* have them put it on right away. My neophytes are dripping wet and need a complete change of clothes. I ask the godparents to present the garments to them, and then let them get dressed after confirmation. Changing clothes right here may unduly prolong the service.

Of course, you're free to have the neophytes slip into their garment if you like. It may not take much time especially if you baptized by pouring, and the brief ceremony can be effective.

230. You invite the godparents to light candles from the Easter candle. You either touch the Easter candle or hold it in your hands, probably depending on the size of the candle.

The godparents light candles and present them to the newly baptized, while you proclaim the pertinent text. The newly baptized are supposed to answer "Amen," but they probably won't know to do this.

To expedite matters, I sometimes have the godparents light the candle as soon as each baptism finishes. So when the first newly baptized person steps away from the font, the godparent, who is holding the garment in one arm, lights a candle with the free hand, and stands with the neophyte while I baptize the next person. Then when all have been baptized, I recite the texts for the white garment and the candle.

Use nice candles. The newly baptized may want to keep theirs as a memento of the night, perhaps lighting it again on the anniversary of their baptism or other special occasions at home.

In brackets are some rubrics for what to do if the celebration of confirmation is deferred. The only ones whose confirmation is to be deferred are infants you may baptize—any child who is not yet old enough for First Communion. You confirm everyone else. There is a provision for deferring the confirmation of adults you baptize (24), but it is for "a serious reason" and the example given is a deferral to Pentecost, not a deferral of several years.

In some parishes practicing immersion, the newly baptized leave immediately to dry off and reclothe themselves. The presider fills the time by advancing the renewal of baptismal promises for the assembly; see 237– 240. I think this breaks the important connection between baptism and confirmation, and introduces an unnecessary adaptation. But others do it.

For some reason, the ephphetha rite, which precedes the baptism of adults, follows the baptism of infants. Except at the Vigil, where the Missal now asks that it be omitted (52). This is probably because people would not understand why infants get it and adults do not—unaware that adults did receive it earlier in the day.

231 [Missal 52-53]. You confirm the newly baptized. People may sing a song before you get underway. It is not critical, and if everyone is ready for confirmation you may start without delay. But the right song might help turn everyone's attention from one part of the ritual to the next. It doesn't have to be long, but a song could help set the stage for confirmation. It's not a processional song; you are not moving anywhere.

You celebrate confirmation in the same place where the baptisms occurred. The Missal says you process to the sanctuary and confirm there, but it refers you to the *RCIA*, where you have the option of confirming at the font. This keeps the sacrament in view of the assembly, and it sends a ritual cue uniting the two sacraments. Their conjunction shows the link between the mission of the Son and the outpouring of the Spirit (215).

232. The minister of confirmation is the minister who just baptized. Whether you are a priest or a bishop, you confirm those you baptize, linking the two sacraments again. At the Vigil, a bishop should not confirm those a priest has baptized; a priest *may not* confirm those a deacon has baptized (*CCL* 883/2). The ministers should be the same, showing the unity of the initiation rites. Exception is made when the number of confirmations is large; in that instance the minister of confirmation may associate other priests with him for this work. This makes more sense if the minister is the bishop, but it does not exclude the possibility that more than one priest will be confirming the group at the Easter Vigil. Normally it is best if one priest can do it all; especially if this is the pastor, he will symbolize his role in the initiation of new members to the community, and in the conferral of the Spirit throughout the flock entrusted to his care.

233. You address the newly baptized, explaining the meaning of confirmation. I usually keep this very brief and move directly into the celebration of confirmation. If other priests are helping you, they stand near you now.

You address the people with your hands joined, asking them to pray that the Holy Spirit will strengthen the newly baptized and anoint them to be more like Christ. This summarizes the purpose of confirmation. Upon hearing your words, everyone prays in silence.

234. You stretch your hands out over the entire group and say the prayer of confirmation. If other priests are assisting they join you in the gesture but not in the words. You are the presider, and they are assistants.

This paragraph bears the title "Laying on of Hands," but as you see, the rubrics never ask you to place hands on anyone. If it can be done conveniently, it would be more expressive for you in silence to place your hands on the head of each one to be confirmed. This gesture goes all the way back to the Acts of the Apostles, and it signifies the conferral of the

Holy Spirit. The rubrics ask the minister to impose hands on the head whenever confirmation is administered to individuals, rather than in a group. See the "Reception of Baptized Christians into the Full Communion of the Catholic Church" (493, p. 137) and the "Christian Initiation of Persons in Danger of Death" (390, p. 130). So it is a most fitting gesture to use.

Just be sure everyone can see what is going on. If the font is in the sanctuary, I usually have the newly baptized stand in a line facing the assembly. But if people are gathered at a more central font, you could stand the neophytes in a circle around it. Everybody should be able to see somebody. I approach them one by one to impose hands. Then I go back to my place and stretch my hands out over the entire group while saying the prayer.

235. A minister brings you the chrism. Anyone may do this. I usually just have a server do it, but the chrism could be presented by a member of the catechumenate team. It would not be out of line to have this person process up the aisle to help people focus on the next step. But remember that the purpose is purely functional. You just need to get the chrism from point A to point B. And the time between the prayer and the anointing should not be unduly prolonged.

When the bishop is presiding for this liturgy, he hands the chrism to you. I'm sure this feels strange to have so many rubrics pertaining to the bishop all of a sudden, especially because the odds are slim he will be present for your Easter Vigil this year. But there are a couple of reasons for this. One is that he remains the ordinary minister of confirmation. Even when you confirm, you do it with chrism that he has consecrated. The liturgy wants you to remember that. The other reason is that the earliest history of these rites described cathedral liturgies. We know about the practice of the Easter Vigil in the eighth century, for example, because the bishop of the time had enough influence for scribes to record what he did or was supposed to do. What you see in these paragraphs of the *RCIA* is the next step in a tradition of episcopal liturgies hundreds of years old. No one is expecting the bishop to show up wherever there is a baptism, but he showed up on paper in earlier liturgical texts, and he has never left.

The newly baptized go to you with their godparents, but you may go to them. I usually choose the second option, but it all depends on the location of your font, the room around it, and the number of people involved. In a tight space with a number of candidates for confirmation, you may have them stand in place. But try to avoid using the center aisle as you will for Communion: confirmation is to be administered where baptism was, somewhere near the font.

I usually have the godparent hold the candle. The newly baptized should have received the candle from the godparent, but I think it gets in the way when I step up to confirm. So even though the newly baptized have just received their candles, I usually have the godparents hold it again during the confirmations. It minimizes the chance that someone will set the priest on fire.

The godparents place their right hand on the shoulder of the candidate, and one of them tells you the candidate's name. You should know this by now, but we're seeing again the results of the long history of this rite. Bishops confirmed large groups of people at a time, and they needed to be told who was who with every confirmation. So a tradition developed around the godparent telling the bishop the name of the candidate just before he said the sacramental formula. This may still be done, but if you know the names, no one should need to tell them to you.

Also, please note, you are using "the candidate's name." Not some *confirmation* name. In the United States we have a custom of encouraging those to be confirmed to choose the name of a saint under whose patronage they will be placed. It's nowhere in the rite. The liturgical law, canon law, and catechism are all silent on this point. The idea is to confirm using the same name used at baptism to unite the two sacraments. The point of confirmation is not to confer a new name on a person, but to use the baptismal name while conferring the gift of God's Holy Spirit. People still pick confirmation names. Many catechists, parents, priests, and bishops encourage it, but I think it is a bad idea, and it is supported nowhere in the universal legislation of the Catholic Church.

You dip the thumb of your right hand into chrism and make the sign of the cross on the forehead of the one being confirmed while you say the formula. I usually do a little more. I pour a few tablespoons of chrism directly on top of the person's head, and then use my hand to rub it around and make a cross on his or her forehead. I've seen one bishop rub the chrism onto foreheads in a circular motion. I've seen a priest pour nearly a cup of chrism on the head of each candidate.

Be sensitive to a few things here. First, you must trace the sign of the cross on the forehead of the one being confirmed. That is an explicit part of the liturgy and history of this sacrament. The use of chrism is not scriptural, but it evolved from scriptural metaphors very early in confirmation's history. Next, if you want to use more chrism, figure out what works best. The experience should be pleasing for the one being confirmed. If chrism rolls into and burns their eyes, you have set off another whole range of symbols for the meaning of this sacrament (and perhaps a lawsuit or two). You also want to avoid making it look as though you are anointing the *crown* of the head. That is where the postbaptismal anointing now reserved for infants is applied. If you were doing that, you'd use the other text about the priestly anointing of Christ. This is confirmation, and it belongs on the forehead. Work out your technique. Tell your elect about it before the Easter Vigil, and visit with them afterwards to hear their testimony about what they experienced.

According to Pope Paul VI's Apostolic Constitution on Confirmation, the sacrament is conferred "through the anointing with chrism on the forehead, which is done by the laying on of the hand" together with the words. He envisioned that your hand rests on the head of the candidate while you anoint the forehead with your thumb. That's the imposition of the hand.

The newly confirmed answer, "Amen". Someone should tell them about this beforehand, so that they can make the appropriate response at the proper time. You then say, "Peace be with you," and they respond, "And with your spirit." Incidentally, this is the only time that a *priest* uses these words of greeting. Normally "Peace be with you" is reserved for a bishop. But you are acting in his stead, even in the way you greet a faithful Christian. And with confirmation you are bestowing Jesus' own gift of peace; see John 14:26–27.

I cannot resist offering a gesture to go along with these words. I usually embrace the newly confirmed. They have come through so much, and this is the end of this stage of their initiation rites.

In a similar vein, after the last confirmation, I usually say something like, "Congratulations to all of you," which elicits a round of applause from the assembly of the faithful. I find that the people want to express their joy and delight as well, and this is a simple way of doing it.

If I have administered baptism by immersion, and if the newly baptized have been standing around dripping wet through all of this, I send them off to change. They go to the sacristy, the school, the office, the rectory, or some other convenient room, and they are told to towel off and get dressed quickly. We protect the floor of the sanctuary with all-weather carpet or plastic sheets. The newly baptized walk a path to drier ground.

236 [Missal 55]. The renewal of baptismal promises comes next. The baptized will be led to their places among the faithful after that. If you have administered baptism by pouring, you may keep the newly baptized at the font during the renewal. They serve as a symbol for this activity of the faithful. Then the godparents will bring them to their places in the assembly.

A bracketed comment says the faithful do not renew their baptismal promises at a celebration of adult baptism apart from the Easter Vigil. The same is true when you baptize infants outside of Sunday Mass. But if you are baptizing adults at a Sunday Mass, the creed may logically be replaced with the renewal of baptismal promises.

237. At the Easter Vigil you ask the entire community to renew its baptismal promises. All should hold lighted candles. This always takes a little while, so I sometimes cue a few people to start lighting candles just before the confirmations are completed. That way we can begin the next stage of the liturgy without a lag. An Easter Vigil is long, and it should be. But it doesn't have to have long periods of waiting. I think an element like relighting candles can overlap the final confirmations without damage to the concurrent symbols, and it drives the liturgy on.

Anyone can relight candles. You may do this, the servers may, or some other group among the faithful. All fire should derive from the blessed fire of the beginning of the liturgy. You can get it from the Easter candle, but by now all the altar candles are ablaze with blessed fire. Several candle-lighters can begin simultaneously.

In my parish the Fourth Degree Knights of Columbus attend the principal liturgies of the Triduum in their ceremonial attire. I ask them to relight everyone's candles. Their action shows their commitment to holding and spreading the faith. You don't have to do it this way; I'm just indicating that there may be some people in your community who could lead this step in a way that adds meaning to the ritual, that expresses their own ministry as Christians, and that keeps the ceremony moving along.

You give an introduction. A sample is provided. I usually keep this very brief and direct. People have just heard the baptismal promises many times, once for each person being baptized. So I say something such as, "Now I invite all of you to renew your promises." But the text provided in this paragraph is good. It makes the connection between the penitential practices of Lent and the renewal of baptismal promises. Just as the elect underwent the scrutinies during Lent to purge what was evil and strengthen what was good, so the faithful underwent penance during Lent to accomplish the same goal. Just as the scrutinies reach their climax in the making of baptismal promises, so the penances of Lent reach their climax in the *renewal* of baptismal promises. The significance of this moment may otherwise be lost on the faithful. For those who made a real commitment to Lent this year, the annual renewal of promises at the Vigil is the goal toward which those disciplines have tended, a triumphant moment of faith. Lent has renewed us. Once again we turn away from sin, and ally ourselves with the saving grace of Christ.

The rubrics explicitly mention that the candidates for reception into the full communion of the church renew their promises with the faithful. This sentence doesn't belong here. This paragraph should concern the Easter Vigil for groups in which there are *no* candidates for reception. But the paragraph appears to have been copied over from the parallel one in the combined rite (580) without any editing.

238. You ask the faithful to renounce sin. A revised translation appears in the Roman Missal. This is frustrating because the faithful will be "renewing" promises that are different from those the elect were "making". Eventually, the translation of the RCIA will be revised too. You still have two options for the renunciations. If you do the first, people will catch the difference in translations; if you use the second, it will just sound like a slightly different set of questions. The conference of bishops may introduce different renunciations, but this is rarely done.

239. You ask the faithful to profess their faith. These translations are also slightly revised, so they won't align exactly with the baptismal promises in the RCIA. Everyone should respond with a resounding "I do" to each query.

240 [Missal 56-57]. You sprinkle everyone with the blessed water while all sing a song. You are uniting words and actions. Just as people have renewed their baptism by their profession of faith, now they do so with water from the font.

In some parishes the celebrant does not sprinkle, but invites people to step to the font and sign themselves with water. This has a few advantages. It ensures that everyone gets in touch with the water. In a sprinkling rite, it is quite literally hit or miss. By inviting people forward you fulfill a very human need to get up and move around a little bit during a lengthy liturgy. You also help people make a connection between this gesture and the common one they use upon entering a church— signing themselves with holy water from a stoup as a reminder of their baptism. The difference is similar to the one between immersion and pouring: in the first you bring people to the water; in the second you bring water to the people.

If I have baptized by immersion, I invite people forward to the water and then I go to the sacristy or another room nearby to change clothes. I pull of my wet alb and stole, don dry pants, put on shoes and socks, fasten up the wireless microphone, and slip into a dry alb, stole, and the chasuble.

A procession to the font also gives the newly baptized a chance to finish getting dressed and move around into position to carry the gifts up in procession. One or more songs would fittingly fill the time. You conclude the water rite with a short prayer.

241 [Missal 58]. The prayer of the faithful follows immediately, and the newly baptized should be in the church for these. If they have been dismissed from the liturgy regularly during their catechumenal formation, they now have a place among the faithful whose prayer this is.

The rubrics don't mention the collection, but no pastor worth his stipend will forget it. It happens after the prayer of the faithful as usual.

The newly baptized may carry the gifts to the altar. At any given Mass the gifts are supposed to be carried up to the altar by members of the *faithful*—those who will be sharing Communion. Although it is sometimes tempting to assign this task to children who have not yet received First Communion or visitors from other churches, the symbolic force is stronger when the offering is made by those who will share communion. This should be the first occasion when the newly baptized have this responsibility.

242 [Missal 63]. During the Eucharistic Prayer you may make a special mention of the newly baptized. At the Easter Vigil, Prayer I has two inserts that appear as footnotes. But in the back of the Missal, in the collection of ritual Masses for Christian initiation, you'll find additional texts for baptism. Many priests are so used to offering these prayers without the interpolations that it is hard to remember them, especially at this point in a lengthy liturgy. But it is worth the effort to remember. Mark the place with a ribbon before the liturgy begins and prepare yourself.

Note that you are not supposed to use Prayer IV at the Easter Vigil. The reason is that its preface is integral to the rest of the prayer, and the Easter Vigil comes with its own preface (as do the other days of Lent and Easter).

243 [Missal 64-65]. You offer Communion under both kinds if at all possible. Many parishes do this quite faithfully at every Mass, so this rubric almost seems unnecessary. But there are many parts of the Catholic world where Communion under both kinds is still not offered to the faithful. At least on the day of their baptism and the occasion of their First Communion, the option should be offered to the neophytes, godparents, families, and catechists.

Before you say, "This is the Lamb of God," you are to remind the newly baptized about what they are about to experience. The Eucharist is the climax of their initiation and the center of the whole Christian life. I like it if the neophytes line up for Communion after the Lamb of God. That way they are quite visible to the entire community and to me when I give this admonition. I also like to quote St. Augustine, who encouraged his neophytes to "be what they see." So, I say something like this. "My brothers and sisters who are newly baptized, we now come to the moment you have been waiting for. We too have hungered to have you share with us at this table. What we share here is the body and blood of Christ. It guides us and centers us. It is the reason we live. 'Be what you see, and receive what you are.' Behold the Lamb of God, behold him who takes away the sins of the world . . ."

After Mass, a reception would be appropriate. Even if it is simple, give the entire community the chance to mingle with the newly baptized—and break their fast together.

I f you have catechumens and candidates preparing to become members of your parish at the Easter Vigil, you celebrate this combined rite of initiation. This liturgy is widely celebrated throughout the United States, even though there are many other occasions for receiving previously baptized candidates.

Shortly before the *RCIA* in English went to press in 1988, Rome expressed some concerns about celebrating combined rites of initiation and reception. The ecumenical movement of the twentieth century had made significant progress in recognizing the status of validly baptized Christians of other denominations. Prior to this time, when you received another Christian into the Catholic Church, you baptized conditionally. But if you worked an annulment for someone in the same situation, you presumed the baptism was valid. This pastoral discrepancy called for theological clarification, which in the end affirmed the baptisms of most mainline Christian denominations. This sparked goodwill between Catholics and other Christians and prompted advances in ecumenical dialogue.

Rome was afraid that combining the rites at the Easter Vigil would undo this progress. It would make it appear as though there wasn't much difference between other Christians and the unbaptized. But when it became known that many parishes in the United States were already combining these rites, Rome thought it prudent to publish a combined rite showing how to do it. But it was to appear in the appendix of the *RCIA*, to indicate that it did not share the status of the other rites.

Placing the combined rite in the appendix did little to conceal it. Most parishes turn to those pages for the liturgy of the Easter Vigil, and they presume that it is the preferred if not the only way of initiating catechumens and candidates. However, candidates may be received at any time of year, and the combined rite has blurred the distinctions that should be sharp for those who are already baptized.

Included within the definition of "candidates" are those baptized as Roman Catholics but who never received further formation or the sacraments of confirmation and Communion. *RCIA* 409 envisions that they will receive these sacraments at the Easter Vigil. This is new to the history of the initiation rites. If you intend to confirm Catholics, you need the bishop's permission. Catholic candidates are not to be received into full Communion as other Christians are. Hence the combined rite of baptism and reception does not explicitly address the situation of Catholic candidates. They may be confirmed during it, or in the course of the baptism of other adults, or on a completely different occasion.

Personally, I avoid using the combined rite at the Vigil. I like to receive baptized candidates at other times of the year when they are ready, so that they may come to the Eucharistic table without undue delay. I find that reserving the Easter Vigil for the elect galvanizes the imagery of that night: resurrection, baptism, confirmation, and Eucharist.

But the combined rite is in the book and you may use it. Many parishes have been using it profitably for many years.

Incidentally, the *Roman Missal* assumes that you have no candidates for reception. It places the confirmation of the newly baptized before the renewal of baptismal promises. If you wish to follow the combined rite, you will need to consult the appendix of the *RCIA*.

566. The very first rubric of the combined rite sensitively tries to distinguish the two groups: Candidates are supposed to be seated someplace "apart from the elect." The visual distance should evoke the theological distance between those who are baptized and those who are not.

Your homily is to include reference to baptism and to reception. Quite honestly, I do not always do this. My homily is usually about Easter. It may make explicit or incidental reference to the individuals celebrating sacraments, but I count on the liturgy of initiation to catechize.

567–579. The liturgy of baptism takes place exactly as it does when the rites are not combined (219–230). Only one option for the water blessing is given here because it is the only option offered for the Easter Vigil. The other options appearing at 222 are for rare circumstances when you baptize adults at other times of the year. This combined rite, by design, is exclusively for the Vigil.

The two liturgies are otherwise exactly the same until after the presentation of the lighted candle. At that point, the uncombined rite moves directly into confirmation, showing by place, time, and sequence of steps the close connection between baptism and confirmation. But when you have previously baptized candidates to be received into the full communion of the Church, they must be dealt with first. This interrupts the natural flow of the initiation rites for the elect.

580–583. You ask all to renew their baptismal promises. Everyone should hold lighted candles. The newly baptized have just received their lighted candles from their godparents. Someone should light the candles of everyone else. See the comments for 237–240 above, p. 116.

584. You begin the rite of reception. If baptisms have taken place at the font, you move to the sanctuary. The location of the rite of reception is supposed to show the distinction between catechumens and candidates. It is recommended that the candidates not be near the font. Yes, they are renewing their baptismal faith, but this must not be confused with baptism, which looms so large in this liturgy.

You invite the candidates and sponsors forward into the sanctuary. You introduce the ceremony. A text is provided, but you may use your own words.

Given the freedom here, someone from the catechumenate team or the deacon may call the names of the candidates for you, unless you want to make another distinction between the two groups by having a different voice do this. The rubrics assign this to you because you do it in the rite of reception apart from the Easter Vigil (490). There it forms a natural part of the rite. But at the Easter Vigil, much more is going on, and hearing another voice here could help.

When the candidates and sponsors enter the sanctuary, be sure everyone can see and hear them. I usually have the candidates face the assembly, sponsors standing behind them. It will look more deliberate if the sponsors lead the candidates into the sanctuary.

585. The candidates make their profession of faith in what the Catholic Church believes. They may do this as a group; they need not do it individually. They have just renewed their baptismal promises as a group. They may follow it up with this group statement.

Unfortunately, when this rite takes place at the Easter Vigil, this profession of faith is somewhat detached. The rite of reception was designed differently. It was set up for one candidate to recite the *creed* together with the assembly. This one proclamation shows that there is one faith and one baptism. Apart from the Vigil, the candidate recites the creed, the normal way that Catholics profess our faith, and does not renew baptismal promises, which would too closely resemble the rite of baptism. In that design, the candidate follows up the creed with this profession of Catholic faith (491).

However, in the combined rite, the creed is replaced with the renewal of baptismal promises, the sprinkling with baptismal water intervenes, the candidates are called by name, they enter the sanctuary with their sponsors, and they hear an introduction to the next part of the ceremony. This breaks the close link between the common profession of baptismal faith and the individual profession of Catholic faith. It is another reason why the combined rites at the Easter Vigil are not ideal for the reception of baptized Christians into the full communion of the Catholic Church.

586. You pronounce the act of reception. You do this individually, not over the entire group. You call them by name. The sponsor stands nearby.

The rubrics say the candidates come to you, but if it works better in your space, there's no reason why you could not go to them.

I memorize this text so that I can look the candidate right in the eye. It is more effective this way. The words are addressed directly to the candidate, and they are the words the candidate has been longing to hear. The moment has arrived. However you do it, make an effort to speak these words with sincerity and warmth on behalf of those who have yearned to hear them.

Regarding touch, you are not supposed to place your right hand on the head of the candidates if you are also going to confirm them. In almost every case, you will confirm. You do not confirm those who are coming from an Eastern Orthodox Church, but their reception should not take place in such a formal setting anyway. Still, I always feel as if I should be doing something with my hands. I usually grasp the hands of the one being received. It helps personalize the moment even more. We join hands, I look them in the eye, and I cannot help smiling as I say this text. Watching the face of the candidate is a wonder to behold.

587. You prepare to confirm. Everyone may sing a song to note the change in rituals. A short song here about the Holy Spirit could set the right tone. But the wrong music may unduly prolong things. The song is optional. It's up to you if you want to include it. See 231.

588. You are the minister of confirmation. If the bishop is present, and if he performed the baptisms, he confirms those he baptized. This happens rarely, of course; see 232. You have the faculty to confirm those whom you baptize and receive into the full communion of the Church, and you must use the faculty for the benefit of those in whose favor it was granted. This includes children of catechetical age. You may have some children in the group who are younger than the diocesan age of confirmation. It does not matter; you must confirm them at this ceremony. Some priests resist this, but it is a good thing. The children will benefit from the gifts of the Spirit throughout their lives (*CCL* 852, 883/2, 885/2).

If there are a great many confirmations, other priests may help. If you are the minister of confirmation, you may delegate them (14). Ordinarily, though, you confirm those whom you baptize and receive.

Some of the candidates may have been baptized *Catholic*; they may not have received further catechesis or the sacraments of confirmation and Communion. You may admit them to Communion, but if you want to confirm them you need permission from the bishop. You must request this permission for each Catholic candidate. Many bishops will grant this, but they do not have to. If they wish, they may retain these confirmations for themselves or defer them to another occasion. Just remember, your catechumenate group may include some who are unbaptized, some who are baptized Catholic, and some baptized in other Christian churches. Of those three groups, canon law gives you the faculty to confirm the first and the third on the occasion of their baptism and reception. You do not have the faculty to confirm the middle group. You need permission from the bishop.

By the way, the occasion makes no difference. These universal faculties do not pertain to the Easter Vigil; they pertain to the ceremonies of baptism and reception. If for some reason you baptize or receive an adult into the Church on a Thursday afternoon in Ordinary Time, you have the faculty to confirm on that occasion. If you intend to confirm a previously baptized Catholic, be aware that some bishops link that permission to a specific occasion such as the Easter Vigil. Know the local rules.

589. You invite the newly baptized and newly received forward with their godparents and sponsors. If you have permission to confirm anyone baptized as a Catholic, you would logically invite them forward at this time. Their names have not been announced. You or someone else should probably do that.

Up to this point, the rubrics have been careful to distinguish the spaces occupied by the elect and the baptized candidates. Now, everyone is baptized, and the rubrics show no interest in distinguishing the groups. Confirmation carries a slightly different meaning for each of these groups. For the newly baptized it is clearly an initiation rite; for the newly received it is part of their transfer to the Catholic Church; for the baptized Catholic it celebrates their coming to deeper maturity in their faith. For all of them, confirmation signifies the gift of the Holy Spirit for the purpose of bearing witness to the faith. These nuances will be lost in the administration of the one sacrament to people on three separate spiritual journeys. It is especially hard to make these distinctions at this point of the Vigil.

You give a brief address to each group. A sample text is provided, but you may use your own words. You invite all to pray in silence. See 233 on p. 112 above.

590–591. You impose hands and anoint the group. See 234–236 on p. 112 above.

592–594. The Liturgy of the Eucharist goes as usual. See 241–243 on p. 118 for comments. Just before the distribution of Communion, when you address the newly baptized, you should also say a few words to the newly received about the significance of the Communion they are about to share.

Christian Initiation of Adults in Exceptional Circumstances (RCIA 340–367)

I f you have an unbaptized adult who needs the initiation rites in a more compressed form, you may use this liturgy with the approval of your bishop, case by case (331 and *NS* 20).

You may also use this rite if someone is in danger of dying. There is another rite for that specific circumstance (370–399), and you may use it in danger of death, but that rite was designed for catechists and laypersons to administer. Even if the person dying is a child younger than the typical age for confirmation and First Communion, you administer those sacraments as well (*PCS* 290, 280).

This rite is for something else, something exceptional, "for example, sickness, old age, change of residence, [or] long absence for travel" (332), but not for someone moving from one parish or diocese to another (*NS* 20). It may also be that the person has an unusual depth of conversion or degree of religious maturity that calls for baptism more immediately (331). It would be most unusual to use this form of the rite. More likely, if you have someone in exceptional circumstances, you would still be able to offer the catechumenate in stages but at other times of year. For example, if you have an unbaptized person who has completed the rite of acceptance but has suddenly been called up to the armed forces, you may want to advance his or her baptism. But you can usually do this in stages. If you cannot, contact the bishop, obtain permission for using the rite for exceptional circumstances, and proceed.

This rite should take place during Mass (338), and it is recommended for a Sunday Mass with the parish community (339). If you do this, it will considerably lengthen the weekly Eucharist, and you may not have the opportunity to alert people ahead of time. That should tell you how exceptional these circumstances should be.

One reason this liturgy is here is that it resembles the way adults were initiated prior to the restoration of the catechumenate. For hundreds of years all the stages of the catechumenate were collapsed into one rite. The same thing still happens with the *Rite of Baptism for Children.*

340. You receive the candidate. See 48, p. 13 above. Note that you will be wearing the vestments for Mass.

341. You greet the candidate, godparents, and friends. See 49 above. There are no sponsors. They are dispensed with. Godparents are needed, and they fulfill the duties of sponsors all the way through this liturgy.

342. You conduct the opening dialogue. See 50, p. 15 above. The naming of the candidate is omitted, probably because you are dealing with one person here who would have been introduced earlier in the liturgy. The rest of the dialogue is in place.

343. You ascertain the candidate's acceptance of the gospel. See 52 option C, p. 17. You are free to improvise your own text here.

344. You elicit the consent of the godparents. See 53. Note that you are talking to godparents, not sponsors, and that you are asking them about the candidate's readiness to be initiated, not just about the godparents' willingness to set a good example. This question is all that remains of the rite of election (131A).

345. You invite the candidate to the Liturgy of the Word. See 60 above. You omit the signing of the senses.

346. The Liturgy of the Word begins. You omit addressing the candidate (61).

347. You may choose readings of the day or those from the Lectionary for Ritual Masses, "Christian Initiation apart from the Easter Vigil" (338).

348. You preach a homily (63).

349. Intercessions follow. These bear some resemblance to those from the scrutiny rites, but they are unique to this liturgy. They may be adapted; the number may be shortened. Note that someone else should lead the petitions.

350. The penitential rite offers a trace of a scrutiny. You may omit it. If it is included, it consists in a general confession of sins. You do *not* conclude with the usual absolution formula from the beginning of Mass. Baptism will take care of all forgiveness of sin.

351. You offer a prayer of exorcism. The text is unique to this rite, though the form resembles the exorcisms from the period of the catechumenate more than those from the scrutinies.

352. You anoint with the oil of catechumens or impose hands. See 103 on p. 35, and *RBC* 50–51 on p. 146.

353. You go to the font and introduce the ceremony of baptism. The litany of the saints is omitted. See 219–220, p. 104.

354. You bless the water. Only two options are given. Choose one depending on the season of the year. See 222, p. 106.

355–357. You invite the candidate to renounce sin and profess faith. See 223–225, p. 107.

358. You baptize either by immersion or pouring. See 226, p. 108.

359–361. You conduct the explanatory rites. The anointing of the crown of the head is completely omitted because you will confirm this person. See 227–230, p. 110.

362–366. You confirm the candidate. References to the bishop tenaciously appear here (363) because he is the ordinary minister of this sacrament. But you have the faculty. Confirm. Note that you lay your hands on the person's head; you do not extend your hands as you would over a group. See 231–235, p. 112.

367–369. The Liturgy of the Eucharist continues as at the Vigil, but without the renewal of baptismal promises and the sprinkling of the assembly. See 241–243, p. 118.

I hope you don't have to face the situation where you need this rite, but if you do, you may and should use it. See the introductory material for further adaptations (332–339). You may expand this with more elements if you wish. The rite tries to make it a little difficult for you because the full catechumenate is usually so beneficial to the unbaptized. Don't rush into this rite, but know that it's there.

Christian Initiation of a Person in Danger of Death (RCIA 375–399)

If an unbaptized person is in danger of dying, you may use this version of the rite. It was written for a lay presider. Ordinarily, a priest is expected to use the rite for exceptional circumstances (331–369). But if you are unable to get the person to Mass, you may use this version. And if death is imminent, just baptize (373).

The person should give you some assurance that if death does not happen, he or she will complete the usual catechesis (371) and other ceremonies (374).

The same rite appears in *Pastoral Care of the Sick: Rites of Anointing and Viaticum* (275–296) with very minor variations. The numbers below follow the sequence in the *RCIA*.

375. You start by sizing up the situation. Visit with the family. Talk to the sick person. Find out his or her motives. If you decide to baptize, give some instruction.

376. Identify a godparent and a witness from among the family, friends, and neighbors; unblessed water may be used. These conditions are relaxed because the rite envisions that a layperson is presiding and no priest is near.

377. You conduct an opening dialogue, keeping it simple. Sample questions are given, but you may choose others. See 50–52, p. 15.

378. You obtain the godparent's pledge to promise, and the support of those who witness this ceremony. See 53, p. 18.

379. For the Liturgy of the Word, you proclaim one Gospel reading. You may choose one from the recommended list, or choose your own. You will need a Bible or Lectionary. Many of these Gospels can be found in volume four of the Lectionary under "Ritual Masses: Christian Initiation Apart from the Easter Vigil." If you are using the *PCS*, see if your edition has a selection of readings in the back of the book.

You "explain" the reading. The word "homily" does not appear here because the rite is written for a layperson. If you are leading it, give a brief homily on the text.

380. You lead intercessions. It would be good if someone else read the petitions. Sample petitions are provided, and these are sensitively composed. Still, they may be shortened or changed. They may also be omitted if the sick person is tiring. Our Church is never shy about praying for healing. Note that one of the petitions is to "restore him/her to health." However, it does appear in brackets, in case it is clear that this will not happen.

381. You conclude the intercessions with a prayer. In brackets again is a request for restoration to health.

382. You lead the shortest version of the renunciation of sin. See 224B, p. 107.

383. The profession of faith may be made in question and answer form, or with the Apostles' Creed. See 225, p. 108.

384. You baptize by pouring. This is the only instance in the contemporary Catholic liturgical library in which immersion is not mentioned. See 226, p. 108. The liturgy imagines that a layperson is baptizing someone who is very sick in bed.

You use "the name the sick person desires to have." In our culture, this is almost always the birth name.

385–388. You skip the anointing after baptism because you are a priest and you will administer confirmation. See 228, p. 110.

389. You introduce the confirmation rite, though you may skip this introduction if the person is very sick (388). See 233, p. 112.

390. You impose hands on the person you just baptized. When you confirm a group, the rubrics have you extend your hands over all of them.

When you confirm one person, place your hands on his or her head. See 234, p. 112; and 493, p. 137.

You say the accompanying prayer. If the person is very sick, you may omit the handlaying and the prayer (388).

391. You anoint the person with chrism and say the sacramental formula, concluding with the greeting of peace. See 235, p. 113. If the person is very sick, and if you want to confirm, you must at least anoint and say the formula (388).

392. If you are not offering viaticum, skip to the concluding rites (399). Only if the person cannot swallow would you logically omit viaticum.

393–394. You begin viaticum with an invitation to prayer. Use option A because you have just offered confirmation. Option B is only said by a layperson, who cannot confirm, and when there is hope that a priest can still arrive before death does.

Lead all present in the Lord's Prayer. Even the most grief-stricken will probably join this prayer.

395. Administer viaticum. This First Communion may also be the poignant last Communion. The rubrics indicate that you use Eucharistic bread. However, it is permissible to offer Communion under the form of wine, especially if chewing is difficult (PCS 74). This liturgy presumes that you are not celebrating Mass, that you have brought previously consecrated elements to the sick person.

After giving Communion, say the formula for viaticum: "May the Lord Jesus Christ protect you and lead you to eternal life."

You may distribute Communion to others. Allow time for silent prayer.

396. You say the prayer after communion. Note again the reference to "healing power." We keep praying for the best results.

397. Conclude with a blessing. Use option A because you are a priest.

398. All may offer a sign of peace to the sick person. In context, this is not just an expression of affection, though it is that. It is the sign exchanged among faithful Christians. At a typical Mass catechumens are dismissed before the sign of peace. The baptized faithful share peace and Communion. See 497, p. 137. This particular sign of peace, though, is borrowed from the liturgy for viaticum (PCS 211), and has more to do with dying than with initiation.

399. The alternative concluding rites are for those circumstances when confirmation and viaticum are not given. This should be rare because you should confirm in this instance.

God willing, you will not be in a situation where you need this rite very often, but if you do, remember that it is here.

When you have Christians baptized in another denomination who wish to join the Catholic Church, you receive them into the full communion of the Catholic Church with this rite. You may celebrate this at any time of year. It is recommended that it take place during Mass, whether with a small group or on a Sunday or solemnity (475/2, 482, 487). *NS 32* prefers a Sunday Eucharist with the assembly of the faithful. The celebration of the sacraments is forbidden on Good Friday and the morning of Holy Saturday. Otherwise, you may celebrate this rite any day of the year.

In the United States it is customary to combine this rite with those of initiation at the Easter Vigil. Parishes typically prepare catechumens and candidates together, and they also combine their rites. It is not forbidden, but combining the rites blurs the distinction between the groups, it may set up unnecessary obstacles for those baptized in other religions, and it may send a confusing message about the validity of baptism. The introduction to the rite cautions that any appearance of "triumphalism" should be carefully avoided (475/2). This fear comes from those who labored hard in the ecumenical movement of the last century. The rite of reception should not look as though we have bagged another heretic. It should pay homage to the spiritual discernment of the candidate, and to the rights that are theirs as a member of the body of Christ. We naturally want to celebrate with those who are coming to communion with us, but it is hard to imagine a more triumphalistic environment than the Easter Vigil. "Anything that would equate candidates for reception with those who are catechumens is to be absolutely avoided" (477).

This rite was originally conceived to take place apart from the Easter Vigil. Those who prepared it kept it simple. They eliminated the requirement for baptized Christians to abjure former beliefs. They gave the priest the faculty to confirm. They set it up so that a person could be received when he or she was ready without any anticipatory rituals. The ceremony is solemn, personal, and simple. The highlight is Communion at Mass, with all its understated wonder.

The adapted rites of welcoming, sending, the call to continuing conversion, and the penitential rite were all conceived for those who were baptized but remained uncatechized, those who "have not yet heard the message of the mystery of Christ" (400). The judgment to use those rites should be made case by case, based on one's catechetical formation (478). These adapted rites may be offered to those being received, but they are not required. All that is required is the rite of reception itself.

I like to celebrate this at a Sunday Mass several times a year, as the baptized candidates complete their formation. Many of them come with plenty of experience in the Christian life. All we need is to confirm their comprehension of what it is to be Catholic, and to verify their desire (477). They should confess their sins beforehand (482). Most baptized candidates do not need to wait until Easter.

One or two persons from the Catholic community should take the role of the sponsor (483). Presumably, the baptized persons already have godparents, but whether or not they do, Catholic sponsors should be identified and ready to help.

By the way, the original Latin of this rite consistently refers to one candidate, not many. The English translation introduced the plural in a number of places, as if you are receiving several candidates. But the original vision is that you receive them one by one, as each is ready.

487. You celebrate this rite within Mass if at all possible. The climax will be eucharistic Communion (475/1), so you want to provide the framework for that to happen. The celebration may be done privately, but I prefer to have at least some members of the parish present. Sundays work best because they give the broader community an opportunity to rejoice with the newly received and to support them with their prayers (NS 32).

You may use the Missal texts from the Mass for the Unity of Christian (Masses and Prayers for Various Needs and Occasions #17) even on an Ordinary Time Sunday, but not on Sundays of the seasons of the year. I would be careful with this. The texts are praying for Christian unity, which is an excellent intention, but the liturgy should not imply that the only path to unity is through the rite of reception. Unity may also be achieved through doctrine, worship, and moral behavior. You are balancing the respect Catholics have for other Christian Churches with an individual's decision to be received into the Catholic Church. Some of the texts for the Mass for the Unity of Christians are more fitting than others; the preface, for example, affirms the unity that exists. You don't have to use these. It may be best simply to use the texts of the day.

488. For the readings, you may choose those of the day, those for the rite of reception (LM 761–763), those from the Mass for the Unity of Christians (867–871) or from the Mass for Christian Initiation (751–755). On Sundays in Ordinary Time you may completely replace the Lectionary readings; on days of greater rank you may switch one of them. I don't advise this because the Lectionary has beautifully crafted the readings of the day. If you want other texts, just be careful in your choice.

489. You preach about the significance of this event. If you have chosen readings from one of the ritual Masses, you will have an opportunity to explain them in context.

The rubrics want your homily to cover a lot of ground: gratitude to God, baptism as the basis of one's reception (probably an allusion to the Decree on Ecumenism 22), confirmation, and Eucharist. I would keep the big picture here and not get bogged down with too many explanations. You should have ample opportunity to catechize on these elements apart from this one homily.

490. You invite the candidate and the sponsor forward. A sample text is provided, but you may use your own words. Could a deacon or a catechist make this introduction? It makes sense for someone familiar with the person's formation to introduce him or her by name to the community. The liturgy has in mind that you introduce the meaning of the rite. But it says you may use similar words, so you are at least responsible for seeing that the right content is given.

One key point in the sample introduction is the phrase "of your own free will." We are celebrating something the person has discerned. That phrase was intended to help avoid the "triumphalism" the rubrics abhor. The candidate comes freely, not as booty.

I usually arrange the candidate and sponsor in the sanctuary facing the assembly. But he or she could also face the same way as the people while reciting the creed in solidarity with them, turning to face them for the profession of faith (491).

491. All recite the Nicene Creed, not the Apostles' Creed. The Apostles' Creed has some affinity with baptism. The Nicene Creed is a more developed expression of our belief and it is the more fitting choice for the rite of reception.

Immediately afterward, the candidate makes a profession of faith in what the Catholic Church believes is revealed by God. I invite him or her to read this off a card. The sponsor may hold it. But the candidate could also read the statement straight out of the *RCIA*. A server could hold the book, and someone could point to the statement. If there is more than one candidate, you could have them recite it all together; provision for that is in the combined rite at the Easter Vigil (585, p. 122).

492. You speak the act of reception. This is a very important moment. I memorize this text so that I can look the candidate in the eye. These are the words he or she has been longing to hear. See 586, p. 123.

You lay your right hand on the head of the candidate only if you are not confirming immediately afterward. You would follow that up with the sign of welcome. This would apply, for example, if you are receiving someone joining the Catholic Church from an Orthodox Church. You are eligible to be the minister in that situation, but the preferred minister is someone from the parallel Eastern Catholic Church. Apart from these rare instances, you will confirm those you receive. So you omit placing your hand on the candidate's head.

The history of this gesture has to do with the reception of a schismatic. It has a certain penitential tone to it, and it is not especially fitting for this celebration. The Catholic Church used to have a rite called the reconciliation of heretics, but that language has been eliminated. The person is being received, not reconciled. Baptized candidates are not being forgiven the "sin" of being members of another Christian Church. They are being received into full communion.

493. You confirm the candidate. You impose your hands on the candidate's head. Normally, the rite of confirmation has you extend your hands over the heads of a group. But handlaying has biblical antecedents, and it is the preferred gesture. See 234, p. 112.

You recite the prayer for the coming of the Holy Spirit. The rubric is not clear, but you are probably supposed to keep your hands on the person's head while offering this prayer. When confirming a number of candidates, you extend your hands over the heads of the group while saying the prayer (234, p. 112). Here you keep your hands on the person's head.

494. You anoint the person with chrism, while the sponsor places his or her right hand on the candidate's shoulder. See 235, p. 113.

495. You give a sign of welcome. It is recommended that you take the hands of the newly received person into your own. The rubric even tells you why: It's a sign of friendship and acceptance. Your bishop may allow a different gesture.

In practice, I usually blend this gesture with the words that conclude the confirmation rite: "Peace be with you." The words and gesture seem to flow well together. I sometimes move from a handshake to an embrace. Whatever you do should feel natural, and it should be an obvious sign of friendship and acceptance.

496. The general intercessions follow. These replace the prayer of the faithful at Mass. If this is a Sunday Mass, you may incorporate the usual intentions from the other Masses at the parish that weekend. You may include a petition for the newly received person at other Masses as well. You are free to compose your own intentions in place of these.

But these are good. Note that the person is called by name in the introduction and in the petitions. Note also that the third intercession is for the Church or community from which this person came.

497. The entire assembly may be invited to extend a sign of peace to the one who is newly received. At first this sounds unwieldy, but I find it works rather well. The rubrics don't say who invites them forward. I usually do it myself, but a deacon would fittingly take leadership here.

In my experience at Sunday Mass, many people leave their places and come to the sanctuary to give a sign of peace. Many others don't. But it always seems to be just about the right number. People who know the person are happy to have the opportunity to step forward. Others come up just to be friendly.

It seems odd that the celebrant's "sign of welcome" is separated from the congregation's "sign of peace" by the general intercessions. The first is supposed to be a sign of friendship and acceptance; the second is a greeting of peace. The first is given by the minister; the second by the assembly. The first seems to complete the rite of reception, whereas the second completes the Liturgy of the Word. According to Justin the Martyr (+ c. 150), the faithful exchanged the sign of peace after the general intercessions and before bringing up the offerings. The sign of peace is a Christian thing to do—it is part of the Mass that comes after the dismissal of the catechumens. But it also gave Christians an opportunity to show peace before making their offering, in accord with the words of Jesus in Matthew 5:23–24.

That is why the rubric says you may omit the sign of peace before Communion; this one is supposed to replace it.

In practice, though, I find these distinctions artificial. Most people coming up to greet the newly received person are doing it with the same purpose the celebrant does: to give a sign of friendship and acceptance. The sign of peace has another meaning. It would have made more sense to allow everyone to give the sign of welcome together with the celebrant at 495, and then let the sign of peace take care of itself as it usually does at Mass. But the rubrics did not give that option.

498. Mass continues as usual. Offer Communion under both kinds.

499–504. You may conduct this ritual apart from Mass, but it weakens the meaning. If you think you have a good reason, though, these paragraphs will tell you how to do it.

Baptism
for Several Children
(RBC 32-71)

When you are baptizing children younger than catechetical age, you use the *Rite of Baptism for Children*. The age group includes everyone from newborns to about the age of First Communion. If a child is older than that, follow the instructions from the *RCIA*.

This was the first of the rites to be revised after the Second Vatican Council. When you read it, you can still encounter the fresh enthusiasm that accompanied the liturgical renewal. A rite for baptizing children existed prior to the council, but it was a watered-down version of the rite for adults. On many occasions the minister addressed the infants as if they were adults, even asking them to make a confession of faith. The new rite treats a baby like a baby. The former rite gave the godparents a more significant role than the parents because the child was often baptized before the mother was strong enough to go to church for the ceremony. Now the parents take center stage.

We baptize children on the assumption that they will later be formed in the faith (3). This formation occurs in the family and in the broader community. You should have some well-founded hope that this will happen before you baptize.

Normally an infant should be baptized within the first few weeks after birth (8/3), though exceptions are made: earlier if the child is in danger of death, later if the family needs more time to prepare. The Easter Vigil and Sundays are recommended for baptism because of its paschal character (9), though the rite cautions not to celebrate baptism at Mass "too often." It promises regulations, but these have never appeared.

Many parishes avoid baptisms during Lent in order to highlight the connection between baptism and the Easter season. This makes Easter a more joyful season, but the universal Church does not forbid baptisms during Lent. In 1988 the Congregation for Divine Worship said that it was not fitting to celebrate baptisms on any of the days of Holy Week (*Circular Letter Paschale Solemnitatis, "On Preparing and Celebrating the Paschal Feasts,"* 27), but it said nothing about the other five weeks of Lent.

If you are celebrating the baptism of infants at the Easter Vigil, parts of the ritual should take place earlier (28/1). This can be done during the preparation rites of Holy Saturday; see p. 93. For adjustments to the ceremony of baptism for adults, see p. 110.

The place of baptism is usually the font of the parish church, though exceptions may be made for architectural, geographical, or emergency reasons. For exceptional reasons the bishop may permit baptism in someone's home, but this is not normal (11–13).

The *RBC* also suggests that adults receive help in tending the children (14), placing the infants in "the care of other women" while everyone else celebrates the Liturgy of the Word. The writers probably wanted to show their concern for everyone, but not many parishes take this suggestion.

If there are very many children and additional priests or deacons present, some of the parts may be divided among them. But ideally, you preside for the entire ceremony (34).

35. All sing a song while you go to the entrance of the church, or wherever the community has gathered. If you are celebrating Mass, you wear alb, stole, and chasuble. If this is a word service, you wear alb or surplice and stole, with or without a cope.

If this takes place during Mass, the entrance hymn suffices for this song. I usually recommend that this music be kept very brief; one verse is probably enough. Sometimes I have omitted it—even at Sunday Mass— because we will be singing a processional song shortly.

Before anything, though, I have the cantor do a brief announcement, such as, "Good morning, everyone, and welcome to St. Aloysius Catholic Church. We welcome today Daniel and Tina Praiswater, who are presenting their child for baptism."

In this announcement, I ask the cantor *not* to mention the name of the child—just to give the names of the parents. The *parents* will give the child's name at the beginning of the ceremony, and they are the ones who should pronounce it first in the assembly.

If this is a single-parent situation, I will still have the cantor introduce the parent. Many single parents want the baptism of their child to take place apart from Mass, to minimize the attention to their family situation. But the parish is responsible for this child, too. If the parent is willing to have a public ceremony, members of the community can be there to express their willingness to help by word and example. Sometimes it is the families in this situation who need the community more than others do.

The parents, godparents, and the child should be gathered by the door of the church, if possible. Some churches have a gathering space or narthex. The liturgy could begin there even for a Sunday Mass. Realistically, it is not easy for everyone to see a ceremony that begins at the door of the church, so audio reinforcement is essential.

36. You greet everyone and introduce the ceremony. The rubrics give you a few ideas for this. The point is to set everyone at ease and give reasons why the Church regards this as a joyful occasion. It helps if you are joyful while you say these words.

37. You ask the parents for the name of the child and to state what they are requesting of the Church. You may need to provide microphones for this dialogue. If you wear a wireless mic, it may pick up the parents' response; but a separate mic for them is better. Just be sure they speak in a loud, clear voice. I sometimes stand a few steps away from the parents so they will more naturally speak up.

You have two choices for your question: "What name do you give?" or "What name *have you given*?" Effectively, there's no difference. But in the first instance, the parents are formally conferring the name of the child in this ritual moment. In the second instance, the child is already known by his or her name. I usually ask, "What name do you give?" to make this a more formal naming of the child. The second question is especially relevant if the child is a couple of years old.

The next question begs for a fuller response than the one suggested in the rite. You ask the parents what they are asking of the Church. They respond with "baptism," but they may choose some other word such as "faith," "the grace of Christ," "entrance in to the Church," or "eternal life." But parents are free to say a little more—to say a lot more. What *are* they asking of the Church? What are they asking of the people of God, the body of Christ gathered here in this particular time and place? I could imagine more elaborate answers, such as these: "A place for my child within a community that shares my values and beliefs;" "People who will represent Christ and nurture my child in the ways of faith;" or "Spiritual support for my child, so that this baptism will continue to bear fruit." You are free to vary the question a bit. The point is to hear from the parents what they want from the Church. Certainly they want a baptism. That should be obvious. But what's under the surface? What have they experienced that they want their child to have?

Most parents will not be able to think this up on the spot. But good baptism preparation can help them think this over before they bring the child to church. What *are* they asking of the Church? Give them a chance to think it over and to compose a statement that they can make before the gathered assembly.

38. If you have many children at one time, you can ask for the names of the children once, and have the parents go down the line calling out the answers one by one. They may all answer the second question together. In this case, you want a short, succinct response: "Baptism".

39. You ask the parents if they understand what they are undertaking, and they say they do. They don't, of course. No parent understands what they are undertaking when a new child arrives. But this question is more about having them accept publicly the responsibility of training the child in the practice of the faith.

If there are several children to be baptized, the parents may respond as a group, but the ideal response is given by *each* set of parents. The *RBC* obtains this commitment from parents at several points in the celebration.

You may adapt the words given in this paragraph. You may explain something else about the responsibility of training children in the faith. At Mass I generally keep this question brief. For example, "In asking to have your children baptized, you are accepting the responsibility of raising them in the practice of the faith. Do you clearly understand what you are undertaking?" Ordinarily that's enough.

40. You ask the godparents if they will assist the parents, and they say they will. Once again, you may use your own words. These questions are designed to distinguish roles. The parents have a primary role in the baptism because they will be raising this child. The godparents have a very significant secondary role, and they are asked to speak up at the very beginning of the ceremony.

41. You address the children and claim them for Christ with the sign of the cross. It may seem silly to talk to a child, but parents do it all the time.

You trace the cross on the foreheads of the children in silence. You don't say, "In the name of the Father" and so on. You just trace the cross. You invite the parents to do the same. You may invite the godparents "if this seems appropriate." It's hard to imagine why this would not be appropriate. In fact, if there are other Christian family members or close friends nearby, I invite them to sign the child on the forehead as well. We are the body of Christ, and we claim the child as one of our own. A non-believer may refrain from participating.

42. You invite the community to take part in the Liturgy of the Word. If you are processing to the place where that will be celebrated, all may sing a song, such as some verses from Psalm 85, a prayer for life and peace.

Your invitation is the cue to the musicians to begin singing. If this takes place at Sunday Mass, the musicians may continue with more verses of the opening hymn.

In any case, you will probably have a procession moving from the door of the church to the seating near the ambo. In some churches, these two areas may be the same, but ideally they are separate, and a procession ensues. The families often come early enough to occupy this seating before the service begins, and then they artificially leave it behind to go to the door of the church, and then take up their seats again. The ideal is that the baptismal party shows up for this service and hangs around the front door until you invite them in at this point. It just doesn't always work out that way.

If this takes place at Mass, the *RBC* says you skip the greeting and penitential act (29/1). This has to be a mistake. Logically you keep the greeting and omit the penitential rite. At Mass, I do it this way: We start with a verse of a hymn. I make the sign of the cross and give the greeting in the back of church, then conduct the dialogue and the signations, and then process up while everyone sings. If the day calls for the Glory to God, we may use it as the processional music. When I get to the sanctuary, I offer the collect of the Mass. If this is a Sunday in Ordinary Time, that prayer may be taken from the ritual Mass for conferring baptism (29). Otherwise, I use the prayer of the day.

43. The children to be baptized may be taken somewhere else until the Liturgy of the Word is over. Not many parishes do this. The idea was to give restless children adequate care, and to let other members of the family hear the Word of God in peace. If you want, you could invite someone else to take care of the kids for a while. But in my experience most parents don't want this. They want to keep the infants with them.

44. You proclaim at least a Gospel. The rubric says "One or even two" Gospels may be read, but this is a mistranslation of the Latin. "One or another" Gospel is more accurate. You read one Gospel, not two.

This may be a full Liturgy of the Word, even apart from Mass. One or two readings may precede the Gospel. A psalm and Gospel acclamation may be sung. It helps to have good readers and musicians on hand for this. If your parish frequently celebrates baptisms apart from Mass, you may want to give some attention to the music ministry. Cantors can enliven these celebrations.

When celebrating baptism at Mass, you will probably use the readings of the day. During seasons such as Advent, Lent, and Easter, *RBC* 29/2a lets you replace one reading, but *CB* 434 says you can't. Or at least a bishop can't. During Ordinary Time or on the Sunday after Christmas (unless Christmas was a Sunday), you may change the readings from those assigned in the Lectionary to those for baptism. The correct numbers in the Lectionary are a bit off those quoted in the *RBC*. You want #756–760. The *RBC* gives the same list at 186–215. There are some minor discrepancies in the translation of the Gospel acclamations and a refrain for a psalm. When in doubt, refer to the Lectionary, which postdates the *RBC*.

So if you are baptizing one or more children at Mass on an Ordinary Time Sunday morning in July, for example, you could change one or more of the readings assigned for the day and replace them with readings from this list. Pastorally this is usually not a good idea because many people— from the musicians and readers to members of the assembly—have prepared for this Mass with the readings of the day.

If you are celebrating baptism at a Mass on the First Sunday of Advent, for example, you use the readings of the day because of the pastoral benefit of the faithful and the character of the season.

When baptism is celebrated apart from Mass, you turn to this list and select readings from it even during a season such as Easter. But it is hard to capture the flow of a Liturgy of the Word with a community that has gathered just for this baptism. The readings usually go more smoothly and integrate with the celebration more naturally if the baptism takes place at Mass.

45. You give a short homily. You should explain the meaning of baptism and encourage parents and godparents to be faithful to their responsibilities. When I celebrate baptism apart from Mass, I usually improvise a brief reflection on the biblical text(s). When celebrating baptism at Mass, I most often preach the homily I have ready for the other Masses that weekend. But you may incorporate ideas about baptism if that is easy for you to do (29/2b).

If baptism will be by immersion, I encourage parents to unclothe the child during or after my homily, and to wrap him or her in a towel or something else that can be quickly removed. Many parents prefer to keep the diaper on until just before the immersion. This has proved wise on more than one occasion in my life.

46. Silence is observed. You may invite this silence after the homily, after the litany (see 48), or *during* the litany. (*GIRM* 71 allows the congregation to respond to each petition in silence, though this is rarely done and could be especially difficult in this circumstance.) However you do it, people should take some time to pray privately and quietly before the baptism takes place. You invite them to do this.

A song may follow the silence. The suggested texts (225–245) are brief. The idea is to sing an acclamation of some kind. People could even sing the refrain of a popular religious song if the text seems appropriate. The point is to focus everyone's attention on the ceremony that is about to happen. If this takes place at Mass, I usually invite the family to the font at this time (but see 52). A song could cover this movement.

By the way, I usually invite small children to the font as well. If it is hard for them to see from their places in the church, I let them come forward and take a seat on the floor. This proximity usually keeps their attention fixed, but sometimes it helps to have a parent or catechist on hand to maintain order.

If this takes place at Mass, the creed is omitted (29/2c). All will be renewing their baptismal promises.

47. You introduce the prayer of the faithful. As always, you have complete freedom in the composition of this text, but several samples are given; see 217–220. Together with the sample petitions in 47, you have an exceptionally generous list from which to choose. You introduce the prayers, but an assistant should read the petitions. At Mass, this usually takes care of itself, but if you are baptizing apart from Mass, it's a good idea to have someone else lead these petitions.

At a Sunday Mass, you may combine these with the regular parish intentions. Or one or more of the parish intentions could be drawn from this list (29/2d). It's a good idea to pray for these children by name at all parish Masses the weekend of their baptism.

48. You invite all to invoke the saints. Although you "invite" all to invoke, you may have the assisting minister or the cantor do the invoking. In many parishes the priest or deacon conducting the baptism reads the litany of the saints, but it doesn't have to be done that way. The traditional ministers of a litany are cantors, so this list could be entrusted to a cantor, reader, or another minister. I usually have whoever is reading the petitions at Mass continue with the invocation of the saints. But a cantor could also lead the singing of this short litany as at the Easter Vigil.

You may include additional saints. For example, the patron of your church or locale could be mentioned by name. If the child has a saint's name, that saint may also be included. A child is not required to have a saint's name. Rather, the child's name must not be foreign to Christian sensibility (*CCL* 855). If the child does not have a patron saint, there is no need to supply one in the litany or in the baptism.

If the children to be baptized were taken out from Mass (43), they are brought back during the litany. Again, very few places send the infants away during the Liturgy of the Word. But if you want, you may. Just bring them back now.

49. You conclude these petitions and invocations with a prayer of exorcism. Two choices are given. Choose only one of them. Both of them refer to original sin. These are the prayers that replace the scrutiny rites of adult initiation; see p. 73. The children are not guilty of personal sin, so the liturgy needs to explain how it is that baptism forgives sin. That is why original sin is mentioned in the *RBC*, but not in the *RCIA*.

The rubrics don't tell you what to do with your hands. Do you use the *orans* position? Do you extend your hands over the children? Do you fold your hands? It doesn't say. Because of the parallel to the first part of the exorcism in a typical scrutiny (see for example *RCIA* 154A, where the prayer is addressed to the first person of the Trinity), you probably hold your hands together. This seems counterintuitive, because you ordinarily extend your hands when you say the prayer that concludes the prayer of the faithful. The rubrics do not say, so you are free to make your own choice. Just have a reason behind it.

50. You anoint the children on the breast while you recite the appropriate text. Use the oil of catechumens. It is sometimes called "holy oil," or *olea sancta*, or even "oil of exorcism." If your vessels are inscribed with a two-letter code, the oil of catechumens is kept in the jar marked

OS. It is usually an olive oil, though any vegetable oil may be used. If you are running low, you may bless more of it. In that case you would replace the prayer at *RBC* 49 with the one at *RCIA* 102B. You don't have to use oil blessed by the bishop for this anointing.

The breast of the child is sometimes hard to reach. I try to anoint the area beneath the neck. If the child is wearing a garment that needs to be loosened, I advise parents ahead of time that I will need access to that area.

51. However, you may skip this anointing. In the United States you may omit it for necessary or desirable reasons. In that case, you have a different text to read, and you lay your hand on each child instead of anointing them. You say the text once, not once per child.

The rubrics don't say where to lay your hand on the child. The head makes as good a place as any.

I often take this option. Baptism comes with plenty of symbols, and omitting the first anointing gives more prominence to the second. It also seems purposeless to anoint children with the oil of catechumens when they will be baptized almost immediately afterward. But the anointing seals the meaning of the preceding exorcism; many priests and deacons like to use it; and it is usually included in baptismal catechesis. You certainly may include it if you like.

52. You go to the font. This procession will be long or nonexistent, depending on the location of this font. In some churches the font is in full view in or near the sanctuary. You won't have far to go. In others it is near the door, still with good visibility. You may have to walk there. In still other churches the font is in a small side chapel, visible only to the few people whom it was designed to hold. That will work if you have a few people at this baptism, but if you are celebrating the baptism at Mass, it will not be a pastorally effective site. You may set up a temporary font in the sanctuary or some other visible place.

All may sing an appropriate song, such as Psalm 23. You see how much this rite expects you'll have musicians on hand. If the baptism is taking place apart from Mass, your musicians will have plenty to sing. If it takes place during Mass, there is plenty of music already. If a verse of Psalm 23 helps cover the procession to the font, use it. If it delays the procedures and hurts the flow of the liturgy, skip it.

53. You introduce the water blessing. Two sample texts are given. Choose one or make up your own. Your words set the stage for the baptism. I keep it brief. We celebrate baptism at Mass fairly regularly, so I can usually get by with a simple introduction such as, "Let us ask God's blessing over the water of this font."

54–55. You bless the water. One option is given here, but be sure you check out 223 and 224 for the other possibilities.

The first option is an eloquent prayer evoking water imagery from the Old and New Testaments. It is a lovely text that deserves to be studied and prayed over. However, in the context of the liturgy, it seems long. Prayed unfeelingly, it will seem to drag on. But prayed grandly, it can effectively set up the seriousness of the ceremonies to follow. You may sing this text if that will add to its solemnity. Near the end, you touch the water with your right hand as you ask the Father with the Son to send the Holy Spirit upon the waters of the font. At the Easter Vigil, that gesture is replaced with the lowering of the Easter candle into the font; see p. 106. For more ordinary occasions, use your hand.

The other two options for blessing the font incorporate acclamations for the people. These have some pastoral advantages: you involve the people more frequently in the prayer, and you break up its themes into sections that can be more easily apprehended.

The blessing in paragraph 223 opens with a trinitarian formula. After you praise each divine Person, the people sing or say "Blessed be God" or some other suitable acclamation. Even if you recite your part, the congregation may sing its response. After this dialogue, you have a choice. In option A you make three petitions to God, after each of which the people sing or say, "Hear us, Lord" or some other acclamation. During your third petition, you touch the water with your right hand.

Option B is for the Easter season. More precisely, it is for the Easter season *when you are using previously blessed Easter water*. If you are using fresh water, use option A even during Easter. But if you are reusing some of the water blessed at the Easter Vigil, use option B, which is a simple prayer. You don't bless over again what has already been blessed.

The blessing in 224 also includes acclamations for the people. It concludes with two options, depending on whether or not you are using previously blessed water. I use 224 a lot when I baptize at Mass. It is brief. It involves the people. The concepts are straightforward. And it helps balance the many important symbols of this liturgy.

The United States Bishops' Committee for Divine Worship has suggested that the blessing of water at the celebration of baptism can be taken from the revised translation in the *Roman Missal* (Newsletter Vol. XLVII November–December 2011:42).

56. You introduce the renunciation of sin and profession of faith. The rubric says you speak to the parents and godparents "in these words"—not in these or similar words. However, many priests and deacons improvise on these. The *RBC* is taking another opportunity to give a strong admonition to the parents and godparents to raise the children in the Catholic faith. The Church wants them to take this responsibility seriously. We all know parents who do not continue to bring their children to church or religious education sessions after their baptism. For some parents the baptism fulfills the expectations of society or of their own parents and family, so they have their children baptized but do not continue their formation. The liturgy of baptism asks them several times about this; see also 39 and 40. If you abbreviate this text, be sure to keep the tone and basic content.

But be realistic. These words alone are not going to improve the religious habits of parents.

57. You ask the parents and godparents to renounce sin. If this takes place at Sunday Mass, you ask everyone to renounce sin with them (29/2c).

You have two options here. The first formula is succinct and traditional; the second elaborates more on the empty promises of sin to which we are sometimes drawn. The conferences of bishops may expand the second formula, but this has not happened in the United States. This option exists in case those being baptized formerly adhered to superstitious and magical practices. In recent history, *all* those being baptized had to renounce such allegiances, even if they never had made them. The renunciation of false worship is no longer an integral part of the catechumenate rites, but it may be included in parts of the world where it is still an issue.

58. You ask the parents and godparents to renew their baptismal promises. A non-Christian parent may refrain. If this takes place at Sunday Mass, you ask the entire community these questions. This will take the place of the creed.

Only one formula is given. If you have it memorized, you can look the parents and godparents in the eye from time to time, and scan the congregation as well. I look at the parents and godparents quite a bit because I want to make sure they are giving these responses. The introduction (56) is supposed to set them on notice that we take these promises seriously. This is their moment to express their faith publicly; they should do so with conviction.

The United States Bishops' Committee for Divine Worship has suggested that the renewal of promises at the celebration of baptism can be taken from the revised translation in the *Roman Missal* (Newsletter Vol. XLVII November–December 2011:42).

59. All give their assent to the profession of faith. You recite a formula, and everyone answers "Amen." In practice, not everyone answers "Amen" because the formula does not elicit the response. If you sing it, or have a cantor assist with the response, you may get a stronger reply.

However, note that some other formula may be used instead. Everyone could sing a verse of a song, or an acclamation of some kind. Musicians can help again.

If this takes place at Sunday Mass, this assent seems unnecessary. After all, everyone has just made the profession of faith. They should not need to affirm what they have just said. The assent pertains more to baptism apart from Mass, when only the parents and godparents have renewed their promises. Then everyone should take the opportunity to voice their assent as well.

60. You invite a family to the font. If there are several families involved, they step up to the font one at a time.

Once again, you ask the parents and godparents to state their intention; see 39, 40 and 56. You baptize only after receiving this verbal and public consent.

You call the child by name. The child need not have the name of a saint. In the past, many priests supplied a Christian name if the parents did not do so. Don't do that. See 48 above, p. 146.

You recite the baptism formula: "N., I baptize you in the name of the Father, and of the Son, and of the Holy Spirit." You may sing it if you wish; some ministers chant it on a single note to add solemnity to the moment. Do not vary the formula. For example, some ministers in other faiths are baptizing in the name of the Creator, the Redeemer, and the Sanctifier. Or in the name of the Father *with* the Son and *through* the Holy Spirit. Or in the name of Jesus, without mentioning the other members of the Trinity. Don't do this. We have a sacramental formula, and if you vary it, you imperil the validity of this sacrament. Know the formula. Memorize the formula. Use the formula.

You may immerse or pour water on the child. Formerly, you were allowed to sprinkle, but sprinkling is no longer considered a valid method for baptizing in the Catholic Church (*CCL* 854). You immerse or pour three times, once after each phrase of the formula. The words and the actions should go together. And you perform all of it. Don't ask a deacon, the parents, or the godparents to immerse or pour while you say the formula. You do it. This is your role. You don't want any question about the validity of the baptism.

For the advantages of baptizing by immersion, see above, p. 108. If your font is not large enough to accommodate the immersion of an infant, you may wish to start discussions on how to remedy the situation. When I baptize an infant, I have the parents remove the child's clothing. I place one hand under the head and another under the child's bottom. I like to receive the child in a way that the head is facing the congregation. I dip the child in the water three times while saying the formula. I do not fully immerse the child; that is, I do not put the face under water. The thought scares me. I get part of the back of the head wet, but in case you're wondering, the Church's law never says that the head has to get wet for the baptism to be valid. I will try to get the child very wet, but I generally keep the face above water.

The parents or godparents should lift the child from the font after an immersion. Once again, you immerse; they do not. But they should receive the child immediately afterwards. They may literally pick the baby up out of the water, or you may hand the child to them after you complete the last immersion. I usually have the parents standing near with a white towel, and I place the child into the towel in the arms of the mother or father.

According to some medieval illustrations, ministers used to immerse by holding the child under the armpits. They then lowered the infant into the water of a sufficiently deep font. You could do this if you want, but I think there are more tender ways to hold a baby.

What if the child urinates? Or defecates? Well, somebody cleans it up. In my experience this is rare. OK, it can happen, but it's not going to happen every time. It is not a credible fear to argue against baptizing by immersion.

If you pour water, the child should be held by the mother or father. This still surprises many Catholics, who expect that the godmother is the one who should hold the child. That tradition evolved at a time when infants were baptized shortly after birth, and the mother could not be present but the godmother could. Now we encourage both parents to attend the baptism. In some cultures the role of the godmother is sealed by having her hold the child at this time. For that reason, it is permitted, but the clear preference is that one of the parents holds the child. This is another way for them to accept their role as the primary teacher of the child in the ways of the faith.

You repeat the question and the baptizing for each child. The people may sing a short acclamation after each baptism. Several texts are proposed in 225–245, but you may also sing a refrain from a more popular hymn, or an alleluia from a Gospel acclamation. A lot of the music at baptisms is optional, but this one seems especially appropriate. It lets the people acclaim what is happening in their midst, and it sounds a note of joy and celebration.

61. If you have a very large number of children, other priests and deacons may assist, and the baptisms may take place simultaneously. But this will probably be rare.

62. You anoint the children after baptism. The text is especially lovely. By the way, the 1990 edition of *The Rites* (Collegeville: Pueblo) has a different translation here. It has adopted the text from *RCIA* 228, which appeared in 1988. However, the Latin texts of the two prayers are slightly different, and the appearance of the *RCIA* should not have affected this prayer in the *RBC*. If you celebrate baptism from a typical ritual book, you probably have the correct translation. Your words are addressed to the children. Everyone is supposed to answer "Amen," but few people know this, and the acclamation is often dropped.

You anoint the children with chrism on the crown of the head. If you have a large number of children, deacons or other priests may assist with this. I usually pour a tablespoon or so of chrism into my hand and then smear the child's head with it. A small dab on the crown of the head will do, but a generous anointing will look and smell more regal. I ask a server to stand nearby with a small towel so that I can dry my hands right away.

63. The infants are clothed in white after you say a text. Everyone is supposed to answer "Amen," but very few congregations do. The text is not written in a way that elicits this response.

The garment is put on at this time. But if baptism takes place during Mass, I have the parents clothe the children after they leave the font and return to their place.

Here's the problem. Most parents bring their children to church dressed in a white garment, a lovely garment, a gown that may have been in the family for generations, one that was shared by many others on their baptism day. To me, it seems superfluous to come up with a different white garment at this time. Some parishes provide bibs or stoles for the child, articles of clothing decorated with some symbol. It seems unnecessary. So in my parish, I ask the parents to bring the children to church dressed in something else. Let me refer to their baptismal garment at this point of the liturgy. They could even hold it up on a hanger for everyone to see. The priest's text (spoken to the children again), says the garment is the sign of their Christian dignity. But they don't have to be wearing it for the words to make sense. Parents could drape the garment over the children at this point. I think the garment has more meaning if the children wear it for the first time *after* they have been baptized. See above, *RCIA* 229.

White is the preferred color. Local custom may permit something else, but white is the color worn by heavenly beings throughout the Bible, and its appearance in this context suggests that the children are sharers in the promise of eternal life.

64. The baptism candle is lighted. You are supposed to "take" the Easter candle while you say, "Receive the light of Christ." Well, some Easter candles are more easily taken than others. At the Easter Vigil, you may touch it if it is too large to hold. Someone from each family lights the child's candle from the Easter candle. The suggested persons are the "father or godfather," but in Latin it could also mean "either parent or godparent." Many parents let godparents take care of the candle, to give them something more to do during the ceremony. The order of persons, however, lists the parent first, but it is probably not a big deal. You may enlist the help of a godparent. When adults are baptized, the godparent fulfills this role; see *RCIA* 230 above, p. 111.

Sometimes it helps to have the *tallest* person in the family light the candle. The lighting of the baptismal candle frequently creates an unintended moment of Olympian drama ("Will the fire transfer or not?"). Just be sure the flame can be reached easily.

You recite a longer text about the fire, and it is addressed to the parents and godparents. Once again, you are reminding them of their responsibilities once the baptism is over. You only need to say the text once. I usually start it while the candles are being lighted in order to cover the time it takes.

65. You may perform the ephphetha rite. It is up to you. You may omit it if you like. You touch the ears and mouth of the child with your thumb while you say the text. You are not instructed to make a cross with your thumb, just to touch the ears and mouth.

The text is slightly different from the one in *RCIA* 199 (see p. 97 above), where it *precedes* baptism. Here the words and actions line up better. You mention the ears and mouth in the order in which you will touch those organs.

All are supposed to answer "Amen," but very few know this and the response rarely happens. Your text does not offer the people a good cue.

66. If the number of children is large you may skip the touching and just recite the formula once. But, of course, you can omit this rite altogether. I generally omit it if I am celebrating baptism at Sunday Mass. It helps focus the celebration on more primary symbols.

If I have celebrated this at Mass, I invite the families and godparents to return to their places. But first I usually congratulate the parents by name, and then say something like, "Welcome, N. and N., to the Christian family!" Usually that triggers a round of applause from the congregation. Not everyone likes applause in church. Some applause is misinterpreted to draw attention to individual accomplishment. But applause can serve the same purpose as a sung acclamation: It lets people exclaim their joy.

If at Mass the families return to their places, they would logically extinguish their candles. The *RBC* implies that the candles burn throughout the Lord's Prayer, but this would not be practical. See below (67–69).

During the Liturgy of the Eucharist, parents and godparents would fittingly carry the gifts to the altar, although the rite does not say this. At the Easter Vigil, newly baptized adults carry the gifts. These children, of course, are too young for the task. But the parents and godparents have been speaking on their behalf, and by having them carry the gifts, they signify their desire to share Communion frequently, to contribute the personal sacrifice required to develop the body of Christ in their children, and to bring them one day to receive the Body and Blood of Christ in the Eucharist.

During the Eucharistic Prayer, the 2002 *Roman Missal* recommends that you use the second Easter preface during that season or the first preface for Ordinary Time otherwise. You also use the inserts provided in the ritual Masses under baptism. Prayers I, II, III, and IV all have special lines for those who have just been baptized.

67. If baptism takes place apart from Mass, you process to the altar. Someone carries the candles for the children, so the rubrics imply that parents and godparents process to the altar as well. If the font is in the sanctuary, this procession will be minimal.

A song may be sung. Once again, the musicians have work to do. The group gathers around the altar, the candles of the newly baptized aglow.

If baptism takes place at Mass, you may invite the parents and godparents forward for the Lord's Prayer, together with the white-robed infants. Music will probably not be necessary, but all may sing an acclamation. The rubrics assume they come with lighted candles, but that means the families need to keep them burning throughout the procession of the gifts and the Eucharistic Prayer. It could be done, but it is impractical.

If you gather the group around you, facing the assembly, it will draw attention to the altar in the midst of the community. In many parishes the baptismal parties remain in their places, but there is good reason to bring them forward. It will alert the community that the initiation of children will eventually include their confirmation and First Communion, and it will remind the parents and godparents that they should continue the religious formation of the children for those events.

68. You lead the Lord's Prayer. You stand at the altar and introduce the prayer. A text is provided, but you may improvise your own. Your text gives catechesis about the three sacraments of initiation. It will then invite all to offer the prayer we always say before communion.

69. All sing or say the Lord's Prayer. If this takes place at Mass, and if the parents, godparents, and infants have joined you at the altar, you may invite them back to their places during the sign of peace. The rest of the Mass continues as usual.

70. You bless and dismiss the community. There are several options for the blessings, and some of these are quite lovely. If the baptism takes place at Mass, these blessings may replace the one for the day (29/5).

The rubric says the mothers hold the infants for the blessing. It would be logical for the fathers to hold the infants for their blessing as well, though the rubrics never indicate this. Perhaps they presume the children will be happier with their mothers—or the mothers will be happier with their children.

71. All may sing a final song of thanksgiving or paschal joy. The Magnificat is one recommendation. When baptism takes place apart from Mass, all may conclude the liturgy with one voice.

The baptized children may be brought to the altar of the Blessed Virgin where this is the custom. The practice is not much observed in the United States. Most new churches would not designate an "altar" for the Blessed Virgin, though they probably have a shrine or at least a statue.

Baptism for One Child (RBC 72–106)

This rite is identical to the previous one, except for the number of children, parents, and godparents involved. It eliminates references to the possibility of multiple priests and deacons, because there is only one child. It also eliminates the recommendation that the children to be baptized may be carried to a separate place until after the Liturgy of the Word (43 and 48); that is apparently thought to be unnecessary when only one child is involved.

The rite calls for the normal use of the baptistry, not the sanctuary, because it envisions that the group is small enough to fit in a tiny place (89; compare with 52). Still, the sanctuary may be used on occasion. The rite for several children envisions that music may be needed for this procession, and it recommends Psalm 23 (52), but the psalm does not appear in the rite for one child (89).

Baptism for a Large Number of Children (RBC 107-131)

Some accommodations are made when you are baptizing a "large number." How many is that? The rite does not say. But it probably means a potential situation missionaries face, where a priest may be available only rarely, and the number of baptisms is quite large—dozens or hundreds. Most parishes in the United States will not need this rite. But you may find a few of its points interesting. The omissions tell you which parts of the rite are less important than others.

108. In receiving the children, you need not ask for all their names. You may simply ask everyone what they are requesting, and they may answer, "Baptism."

111. When you claim the children for Christ, you make one sign of the cross over the entire group, as if you were giving the blessing at the end of Mass, and you invite the parents or godparents to mark the children's foreheads for you; compare with 41.

112. Only one Gospel is recommended, though others may be used. The one is Jesus' command to preach the gospel to all nations, baptizing in the name of the Trinity. This text fits a missionary setting where the gospel has literally gone out to another nation. The rite recommends one reading, not a full Liturgy of the Word, probably to conserve time. You have a lot of work coming up.

The silence and song that may otherwise follow the homily are not included in this rite; see 46.

114. The intercessions are identical, but the invocation of the saints may be omitted; see 48.

115. After the prayer of exorcism the anointing with the oil of catechumens is omitted; see 49. When you say the text "May you have strength," you extend your hands over the group; you do not impose hands individually on each child; see 50.

116. You go to "the place where baptism is celebrated." There is no reference to a baptistry or a font; see 52. Because of the large number of people, you could be anywhere—even outdoors.

118. The blessing and invocation of God over the water takes the form in which the people make a repeated acclamation. The other options for this prayer are not given (54, 223). In theory, you could use them, but the liturgy seems to want to engage the large crowd. That can be done more easily here with acclamations than with a lengthy soliloquy.

124. During the baptisms, everyone may sing acclamations or hymns, or passages from scripture may be read, or sacred silence may be observed. It is expected that this will take a while, even if several ministers are helping.

125. Surprisingly the anointing with chrism may be omitted, in which case the text is amended; see 62. This saves you from going back to all those you just baptized to anoint them individually. In the United States, however, this is not permitted; you must anoint every child.

127. For the lighting of the candles, you recite the two halves of the text at once, not waiting for the action to take place; see 64. What happens next is not clear from the English translation, but I think the Latin has in mind that the head of one household lights candles from the Easter candle, and the burning candles are then distributed to individual families. A song helps fill the time.

The ephphetha is omitted (65). All process to the altar, unless they are already in the sanctuary. The lighted candles illumine the way.

130. A brief blessing is recommended. All may sing a final song. The optional practice of bringing children to the altar of the Virgin (71) is omitted altogether.

Bringing a Baptized Child to the Church (RBC 165-185)

This rite is for the child who was not expected to live, was baptized, recovered, and now is coming to the church for the rest of the ceremony. Normally you don't baptize children outside of the full ceremony of baptism, but in emergencies it is appropriate to do so.

I'll go out on a limb here. I would not use this rite in the case of a child baptized at home by the grandmother who was upset that the parents didn't have the child baptized yet. We baptize infants at the request of the parents or guardians, and it was obviously not their will to have the child baptized at home. Furthermore, baptism by someone other than a priest or a deacon may only happen in case of emergency. Anyone can baptize, but the conditions have to be right. In my opinion, the conditions are not right when a well-meaning person takes it upon himself or herself to baptize at home. If I learn that the child I'm about to baptize has already been "baptized" by a family member at home, I won't use this rite of "bringing a baptized child to the church." I'll use the full rite of baptism for children.

But if *you* or someone else baptized the child because you, he, or she didn't know if the child would live, and if the child *does* live, then give thanks to God, rejoice with the family, and have them bring the baptized child to church. Conduct this rite.

166. In your introductory comments, instead of saying something about the meaning of baptism (see 36), praise the parents and godparents for having the child baptized, thank God, and rejoice with the parents over the child's health.

167. You ask what name the child has been given. The child has already been baptized by his or her name, so the question is in past tense; see 37.

Notice how the second question has changed, too. When you ask what the parents want, they cannot respond with "baptism," so they say they want everyone to know that the child has been received into the Church. Parents would really have to rehearse this line in order to say it. It would be good to let the parents prepare their response. They may want to say something more thoughtful and inspiring, and they are free to do so.

168. Instead of asking the parents to accept the duty of raising the child in the faith, you remind them that coming to church today expresses their willingness to do this; see 39.

169. You ask the godparents to accept their responsibilities. This question is nearly identical to the one in the full rite of baptism; see 40, 78. The godparents are assuming their role in this liturgy.

170. You sign the child with the cross. You recite an adapted text acknowledging that baptism has already taken place; see 41.

171. You invite all to take part in the Liturgy of the Word; see 42. As usual, this may include a procession.

172. For the scripture readings, the same choices remain, but this rite allows two additional possibilities, both about miraculous healings. The first is 1 Kings 17:17–24 (*LM* 90, Tenth Sunday in Ordinary Time, Year C.) The story tells how Elijah restored to health the only son of the widow of Zarephath. The other selection is 2 Kings 4:8–37, which does not appear in the Lectionary. You can get most of it by starting with *LM* 97, the Thirteenth Sunday in Ordinary Time, Year A, and continuing with *LM* 250, the Optional Mass for the Fifth Week of Lent, but it will be easier to proclaim it from a Bible. In this case Elisha restores a dead boy to life. You may choose other readings, depending on the needs of the parents.

173–174. You preach about the significance of these events. You allow time for silent reflection or a hymn. See 45–46.

175–177. The intercessions and the litany take place as usual, but the exorcism, anointing, and blessing of water are omitted. In place of these you offer a prayer of thanksgiving, in which you ask God to continue to protect the child. The renunciation of sin, profession of faith, and baptism are all omitted. See 47–60.

178–180. The explanatory rites continue as usual. This is the main reason the child is coming to church: to be anointed with chrism, to receive the white garment, and to glow in the light of the Easter candle. The ephphetha is omitted. See 62–66.

181–184. The rest of the rite flows as usual. At this point the child is caught up with all the missing rituals. See 67–71.

185. You may adjust the explanations, readings, petitions and other parts of the rite to suit whatever circumstances caused the child to be baptized earlier.

Confirmation of a Person in Danger of Death (PCS 236–258; RC 52–56)

Normally, the only time you celebrate the rite of confirmation apart from the initiation or reception of adults is when an unconfirmed person is dying. This rite, chapter IV in the *Rite of Confirmation*, is one you should know about. Be aware of another solution, though, the Continuous Rite of Penance, Anointing, and Viaticum from *PCS* 236–258.

(Sometimes the confirmation candidates in my parish will ask if there's any way they can be confirmed without having to go through all the requirements. I say yes; all you have to do is start dying, and I can confirm you right away.)

Seriously, only the gravest situations will call for you to confirm a person in danger of death. You should be ready to assist the one who is dying, as well as the family and friends who are grieving.

Let's start with the text in the *PCS*. This suits the circumstance where a baptized person is now in danger of death, but you have time for a fairly elaborate ceremony. You size up the situation and make abbreviations as you see fit (237). It is permissible, though not advisable, to celebrate the anointing of the sick and confirmation in the same liturgy.

239. You greet everyone with a liturgical formula. If you've brought Communion, set the container on a table nearby so everyone may adore the presence of Christ.

240. You give an instruction about the sacraments you will celebrate. You may read a short text from the Gospels. The two suggested are Matthew 11:28–30 (the ease of the yoke of Christ) and John 6:40 (the promise of being raised on the last day). Or you may skip the scripture and speak the suggested instruction. You may even use your own words.

241. You may celebrate the sacrament of penance. The sick person may confess sins even in a generic way, and you offer the words of absolution in the usual way.

242. If you do not celebrate the sacrament of penance, you lead a penitential rite such as those from the beginning of Mass. Suggested formulas are at 118, though this rite omits the reference to the second option, which opens with a proclamation of Jesus who heals the sick. Jesus indeed heals the sick, but the nature of this rite is that we're not even hoping for that right now.

243. You give the apostolic pardon from 201. This is one of the main reasons people want a priest with them when they die. You offer not just forgiveness of sins, but also release from the punishments associated with them.

244. If the sick person is able, you invite him or her to renew baptismal promises. The text is at 190. You sprinkle him or her with holy water after this profession of faith.

245. You lead a litany. Samples are provided, and you may adapt them.

246. If the person has not been confirmed, you administer that sacrament. See comments at *RCIA* 362–366 above, p. 128.

247. If you have administered confirmation, you omit the handlaying for the anointing of the sick.

248. You say a prayer of thanksgiving over blessed oil or say a short prayer blessing the oil.

249. You anoint the sick with blessed oil.

250. You offer a prayer, but you skip this one if you are going to offer viaticum.

251–254. You conduct the liturgy of viaticum. You lead the Lord's Prayer, you give Communion and use the formula for viaticum at 193.

You cleanse the vessels and observe a time for silent prayer. You say a concluding prayer from 209.

255. You bless the group. If some of the blessed sacrament remains, make the sign of the cross with it while holding the pyx in your hand.

256. All may offer the sick person a sign of peace. This is a sign of unity and support with that person. Its purpose differs slightly from the sign of peace at Mass, which prepares the faithful for Communion.

257–258. Whether the person recovers or dies, offer fitting pastoral care.

The foregoing liturgy falls within the *Rite of Pastoral Care of the Sick*, but an emergency confirmation also appears within the *Rite of Confirmation*. You have a choice, and you decide based on the circumstances at hand. If you choose the *RC*, here is what you'll find in chapter IV:

52. You should give some catechesis ahead of time. The person is dying, so don't expect too much. But he or she should have some understanding of what is about to happen, unless, of course, the person is an infant or young child. In that case, it suffices to have the consent of the parents.

Note that confirmation is not supposed to be celebrated together with anointing of the sick. However, *PCS* 238 and 246 allow you to do it, provided you do not impose hands while anointing the sick. By omitting the sacrament of anointing the sick, you avoid the use of two oils, the meaning of which could otherwise be obscured. But we may use two oils when we baptize infants, and that has not been much of a problem. More importantly, the anointing of the sick is a prayer for healing, a prayer for recovery. The confirmation of the dying acknowledges that the person is passing over from this life to the next. It is at some cross purposes with an anointing, though you may do it especially if the person has received neither sacrament. Confirmation of the dying will fit beautifully with viaticum.

53. When possible, do the entire rite of confirmation (20–33). This could even include Mass.

[20.] Choose readings from the Mass of the day or *LM* 764–768 (not 763–767, as the *RC* has it).

[21.] The rite calls for a formal presentation of the candidates, but this person is dying, and you know who he or she is. Nothing special needs to happen here.

[22.] The sample homily is a well-crafted piece of catechesis. It can be helpful as part of the catechesis in 52, but it could be too lengthy and dense to serve effectively when the candidate is this sick.

[23.] You renew baptismal promises. This is a good piece to include. It links confirmation with baptism, and it demonstrates the fulfillment of the canonical requirement that those being confirmed be able to renew their baptismal promises (*CCL* 889/2).

[24.] You invite everyone to pray.

[25–27.] See 54–56 below.

[28.] Assisting priests receive chrism from the bishop. This does not apply under these circumstances.

[29.] All may sing a song while you wash your hands.

[30.] You lead the general intercessions. An assistant may read the petitions.

[31–34.] You continue with Mass, offering Communion under both kinds and a special blessing. If you are offering Communion, do so under the form of viaticum (*PCS* 192–193).

54. But in necessity, you only have to do the essentials. Impose hands and recite the prayer of confirmation while you do so. The person should answer "Amen," if he or she is able.

55. You cross the forehead of the person with chrism while you recite the sacramental formula. If able, the person answers with another "Amen."

You may add other parts of the ceremony if you like. It all depends on the circumstances. You may start with the full rite and eliminate some of its pieces, or start with the brief rite and add to it. Either way, it will work.

56. If you don't even have time for that much, at least anoint and recite the sacramental formula. That's the absolute minimum for a valid confirmation.

First Communion
(LM 769)

 One of the most memorable of all Catholic ceremonies is First Communion, yet it does not exist in any Catholic ritual book. After the baptism of a young child, parents, godparents, and guardians are expected to continue the religious formation of the child, preparing for the first reception of Communion. But the tradition behind elaborate First Communion Masses was a grassroots effort that spread without the guidance of any liturgical document from Rome.

Open volume four of the Lectionary and turn to the Ritual Masses. The first section is devoted to Christian Initiation, and the fifth part bears the title "First Communion for Children" (769). The Lectionary was published in the year 2000. That is the first time in the history of Catholic liturgical books that there is even a *heading* for First Communion. Turn to that heading, and you will find no readings, only a rubric, suggesting that you use readings from the rites of initiation (751–755) or the votive Mass for the Eucharist (976–981).

But that's it. There are no guidelines for processions, clothes, songs, or extra rituals. It has all developed by custom. There will be variations from one country to another, one region to another, even one parish to another and one *pastor* to another within the same parish. On one hand, it is encouraging to see that such an important moment in the life of the faithful has taken hold of the Catholic popular religious imagination because of the efforts of local churches. On the other hand, the variations in custom are more evident in a communication-happy culture like ours, and one wonders if some guidance from Rome might not help. As of now, you can avoid apodictic sentiments that First Communion *has* to go this way or that. It doesn't. You want to help families step into a stream of tradition, but you don't want to legislate so much that the ceremony becomes oddly fixated on its details instead of its meaning. You've presided for weddings; you know what I mean.

So, first things first. Dress. All right, it isn't the most important thing, but it is the thing that will disturb your peaceful sleep unless you manage it. There are no rules governing First Communion dress. None. Girls do not have to wear white dresses, gloves, and a veil. Boys do not have to wear suits. It's about Communion, not a photo op. But it's also a formal occasion steeped in tradition, and many parents want their children dressed accordingly, and many children look forward to dressing up.

Some people assume that the white dress recalls the baptismal gown, thus linking First Communion and baptism as initiation rites. Nice theory, but I don't buy it. First Communion dresses came into vogue in the nineteenth century when the age for First Communion was around twelve, and there is no evidence that pastors, parents, or theologians of the time saw this as an initiation rite. They always saw it as a post-catechetical event: a puberty rite, a rite of moving beyond the world of students into the world of adults. The girls' dresses resembled wedding dresses, not baptismal gowns. They were virginal outfits donned by those entering the nuptial feast of the Lamb of God.

Besides, there is no consistent history on the color of boys' outfits. Some have worn white, but not all. If the First Communion dress were truly a revivified baptismal garment, boys would have sported the same color.

When the age for First Communion dropped in 1910, everything went with it: the catechesis, the liturgy, and the gowns. The wedding outfits looked incongruous on seven-year olds, but the custom stuck because people had a mental image of what First Communion should look like.

Don't get me wrong. First Communion is a formal occasion, and I think kids *and families* should gussy up for it. But if a girl chooses not to wear a white dress, it is not going to spoil the festivity at the heavenly banquet.

A more substantial question is the setting for First Communion. Many parishes schedule special First Communion Masses. They prepare the children for this day through catechesis, and then the class celebrates together. This is the classic First Communion tradition. But some parishes are questioning it. Yes, a child completes catechesis in a class, but aren't the family and the parish community a more appropriate context for celebrating the Eucharist? Consequently, some parishes include First Communion at a regularly scheduled Sunday Mass. Children come in small groups, not necessarily with the entire class of communicants. In this way, a child receives First Communion with the family, not with classmates, and in the context of the full parish community, not of an educational community. It can work either way, but you should know you have some options.

Incidentally, there is a small debate over which is the more appropriate name for this ceremony: First Eucharist or First Communion? The Lectionary now says "First Communion," and I think this is the right choice. The child has been participating in the Eucharist already—attending Mass, hearing the readings, singing songs, and praying with others. But this is the first time the child shares Communion with everyone else. That's what gives the day its distinction.

You may want to revisit the *Lectionary for Masses with Children* and the *Directory for Masses with Children*. The latter concerns children who have not yet entered the period of preadolescence (6). The directory distinguishes between Masses with adults in which children also participate and Masses with children in which only a few adults participate. More accommodations are expected of the second setting, but with the bishop's permission, those may be applied to the first as well (19).

Children may be involved in decorating the church and altar (22, 29). They may join the entrance procession (34). They may sit in any space where they will feel more at ease (25).

You may employ "free use of introductory comments" (23). You may address the children in the introduction to the Mass (17). The act of penitence may be omitted or expanded (40). The text of the Glory to God may be simplified (31) or omitted (40). You may choose a different collect if you find one that children can better understand (50), or you may adapt its words to a child's sensibilities (51).

If the readings are not understandable, you may choose others from the Lectionary or directly from the Bible (43). You may reduce the number of Sunday readings to two or even one, as long as you keep the Gospel

(42). Before the readings begin, you may explain them to the children (47). Children may serve as readers (47). Different speaking parts may be distributed among children for the same reading (47). You may replace the singing of the psalm with silence (46). Children may join the Gospel procession (34), perhaps by carrying banners. After the Gospel it is possible for an approved catechist to speak to the children if you find it difficult to address that age group (24). Children may illustrate points of the homily with art (36); you may engage them in dialogue during the homily (48). If only one reading was used at this Mass, a song may follow the homily (46).

The Apostles' Creed is recommended for children's Masses (49). If the children sing the creed, they may use an approved version that does not correspond word-for-word with the customary text (31). Children may illustrate the prayer of the faithful with their art work (36).

Children may join the procession of the gifts (18, 34). After washing your hands, you may address the children in your own words when you invite the congregation to pray (23). You may choose a different prayer over the offerings if the one assigned for the day is hard to understand (50), or you may adapt the words (51).

The same applies to the preface. Before the preface you may explain reasons why we give thanks (22). You may use the Eucharistic Prayers for Masses with Children. The words of the Holy Holy and Lamb of God may be sung with an approved, adapted text (31). You may use your own words when introducing the Lord's Prayer (23). You may omit the entire rite of peace, moving from the Lord's Prayer to the Lamb of God (53). You may use your own words when you invite the children to Communion (23). You may choose another Communion prayer or adapt the one assigned to help the children understand (50, 51). You may make closing comments before the dismissal (54).

Check with the *Directory for Masses with Children* for the precise legislation, but know that you may do things a little differently with a large number of children in the assembly.

Regarding the readings, the ones from the *Lectionary for Masses with Children* may be used on Sundays when a large number of children is present (12), but not on Christmas Day, Epiphany, the Sundays of Lent, Easter Day, Ascension, and Pentecost (13).

Children may serve as readers. Some parishes like to have one of the first communicants do this, but these children have plenty on their minds already. Their role at this Mass is to receive their First Communion;

others may serve as readers. Choosing another child as a reader may be a good idea, but you might train children as readers the same way you train children as servers. It's not for every child. Let a few of them do it on multiple occasions, and train them well. Some children will read better than adults if they are given the right tools.

The same applies to the music. Some parishes like to have the first communicants sing a song as part of the liturgy. Sometimes this is lovely, but a cantor or choir normally leads the singing; that is not the primary responsibility of these children. Certainly they should have a chance to learn the music for their First Communion Mass. And they should sing it during the Mass. If they are processing in, practice having them process in with the hymnal in their hands, singing out loud. When they get to their places, be sure they know where to find the music and to join in the song.

You may direct your homily to the children. Speak in their language, engage them in dialogue, use their images—do whatever it takes to make them feel a part of the celebration. Keep the focus on what is important: the meaning of this Eucharist and its prominence in the weekly life of Catholics.

Try to keep everything light and child-friendly. Families have been looking forward to this day for years. Help them celebrate its joy, and make the children hungry to come back for more.

Afterword

When you celebrate the initiation rites, you engage young and old, rich and poor, healthy and sick in the mystery of the Church's life. You stand in a privileged place.

The liturgical books give us priests much-appreciated guidance. I always approach them with humility and preside from them as transparently as I can. Sometimes we priests get in the way of the liturgy. We mean well, but we say too much, try an adaptation that isn't rooted in tradition, or do something that offends more than it inspires. I'm as guilty as anyone.

Yet with all our weaknesses, God has endowed us with enough wisdom and heart to shoulder this task: to be at the nexus between Christ and the Church. Presiding for liturgy defines who we are as priests, and presiding at initiation rites brings joy and purpose to our work. Through them we serve the people in our flock, and we are ever creating a new generation of Christians to hear and heed God's holy word.

Index of Rites

Notes

Notes

Notes

Fountain
of Life SERIES

Additional Resources in
WLP's Fountain of Life Series:

Apprenticed to Christ
Activities for Practicing the Catholic Way of Life

Chosen in Christ/Elegidos en Cristo
Music for Christian Initiation/Música para la Iniciación
(Two CD set and Music Book)

Enter The Rose
Retreats for Unfolding the Mysteries of Faith for Catechumens,
Candidates, and All Believers

The Fifty Days of Joy
Easter Season Reflections for New Catholics

We Send You Forth
Dismissals for the RCIA

Formed in Faith
Sessions for Inquiry, Catechumenate, and Ongoing Faith Formation

The Spirit at Work
Conversion and the RCIA

Les Enviamos
Para despedir a los Catecúmenos (RICA)

Other resources from WLP to assist in implementing
the Rite of Christian Initiation of Adults:

In Shining Splendor
Easter Season Reflections on the Exsultet

Enlightened by Faith
Prayers for the RCIA Journey

Living the Word
Scripture Reflections and Commentaries for Sundays
and Holy Days

Seasonal Missalette® Worship Resource